TIMES SQUARE STYLE

C0-ASD-755

GRAPHICS FROM THE GREAT

SQU

BY VICKI

PRINCETON ARCHITECTURAL PRESS

WHITE WAY

GOLD LEVI & STEVEN HELLER
NEW YORK CITY

To my beloved siblings, Valerie, Marc, and Michele, who journeyed with me from the Boardwalk to Broadway. – V.G.L.

To my son, Nick, who has always been a Times Square fan. – S.H.

Published by
Princeton Architectural Press
37 East Seventh Street
New York, New York 10003

Published in association with Pamphlet Architecture, Ltd., New York

For a free catalog of books, call 1.800.722.6657.
Visit our web site at www.papress.com.

©2004 Vicki Gold Levi & Steven Heller
All rights reserved
Printed in China
07 06 05 04 5 4 3 2 1 First edition

No part of this book may be used or reproduced in any manner without written permission from the publisher, except in the context of reviews.
Every reasonable attempt has been made to identify owners of copyright.
Errors or omissions will be corrected in subsequent editions.

Editor: Mark Lamster
Design: Chad Roberts / Louise Fili Ltd
Proofreading: Scott Tennent

Special thanks to: Nettie Aljian, Nicola Bednarek, Janet Behning, Megan Carey, Penny (Yuen Pik) Chu, Russell Fernandez, Jan Haux, Clare Jacobson, Nancy Eklund Later, Linda Lee, Katharine Myers, Jane Sheinman, Jennifer Thompson, Joe Weston, and Deb Wood of Princeton Architectural Press—Kevin C. Lippert, publisher

Library of Congress Cataloging-in-Publication Data for this title is available from the publisher.

All images from the collection of Vicki Gold Levi, except the following:

Pages 11, 18, 19, 20, 23, 55, 59 (top right) 82, 87, 93, 96 (top), 101
Images donated by Corbis-Bettmann.

corbis.

Page 15 National Archives and Records.

Pages 16 , 22, 26 (all), 27, 41 (right), 97, 100 Library of Congress, Prints and Photographs Division.

Pages 21, 53, 128 Child's (middle right) Collection of The New-York Historical Society.

Pages 28, 29, 41 (left), 77, 78 (both), 79 (both), 80, 81, 83, 84–85 (all), 86, 88 (top left, right), 89 (all), 90–91, 99, 102, 103 Photofest.

Page 38, Playbill ® used by permission.

Page 40 (middle right) Eric Concklin Collection / Ziegfeld Club Archive.

Page 54 (all) Richard Merkin Collection.

Pages 57 (middle left, bottom left), 58 Rod Kennedy Postcard Collection.

Page 61 (all) KJA Consulting, Orlando, Fla.

Page 105 Culver Pictures.

Page 123 (bottom right) Henry Voigt Menu Collection.

Page 124, The Lobster ashtray (center) Richard Snow.

Page 128 Evelyn Goldberg , Havana Madrid (top left).

Page 128 Arthur Schwartz , Ruby Foo's (top right).

Introduction

Before its demolition in 1975, Ripley's Odditorium, in the heart of Times Square at 48th Street and Broadway, housed the freakiest freaks of nature. It may be long gone, but it is not forgotten. Times Square is still New York's most spectacular freak show. The clash of high and low, of crass and sophisticated, is unlike anything anywhere else in the city. On an island packed with landmarks, Times Square—the cultural core of a city that is the cultural center of the world—owes its epic persona, its style, to a critical mass of tawdry and classy contrivances.

Times Square has long been defined by its contrasts: legitimate theaters and seamy dives coexist on the same dozen or so streets as cool night spots, posh eateries, seedy dance parlors, palatial movie houses, 24-hour adult haunts, midway penny arcades, kitschy souvenir bazaars, houses of ill-repute, and evangelical salvation missions. Times Square has hosted vaudeville, honky tonk, burlesque, jazz, and pop. Sinatra and Elvis both played the Paramount when they were teen idols. Times Square had more speakeasies and lobster palaces than anywhere else in Manhattan. Its luxurious hotels were legendary even in decay (the Astor, Edison, and Taft all exuded a certain regal splendor until their demise), while its SROs were legendarily squalid. Of course, at the end of the day, nothing is more quintessential of the "White Light District" than the high-voltage advertising extravaganzas that from 1905 to the present have unremittingly spewed light, steam, and sound onto Broadway, and keep the area glowing in an unparalleled display of megawattage.

Whatever one's pleasure, obsession, curiosity, or vice, Times Square exerts an appeal; as the world's grandest carnival, it has attracted visitors from the farthest reaches of the globe. Even native New Yorkers admit it is exotic turf—an island on an island—more like a foreign country than an

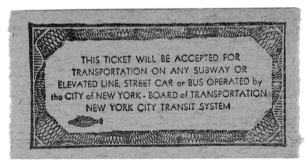

5 CENTS ONE FARE
Paper tickets were used for subways,
street cars, and buses before the token.
Subway Ticket
C. 1940

It is certainly apt as it relates to New Year's Eve, when millions of pilgrims stand huddled together in the frigid air, hypnotically watching as an illuminated sphere (the planet earth?) drops from New York's premier bell tower. It feels as though a quirky kind of religiosity is invested in this place, and if responding to Times Square's otherworldly pull is not some kind of spiritual devotion, then what is?

The original Times Tower, erstwhile home of the *New York Times*, gave the narrow triangle formed by the convergence of Broadway and Seventh Avenue between 42nd and 43rd Streets—originally christened Longacre Square—its name. It was conceived as a cathedral of respectability in the midst of a dubiously inhabited theater district known as the Rialto. (Please further note the curious transfiguration of a triangle into a square). But the entrepreneurs—the Hammersteins, the Shuberts, and the Nederlanders—who

urban neighborhood. Beginning in the early 1900s and through its golden age, no other locale has fizzed with such inexhaustible energy. Even in its days of decrepitude in the 1960s and 1970s there was a besotted buzz about what Times Square was and could be. And whatever one thinks of the recent redevelopment that has made it cleaner, safer, and wealthier, Times Square will always remain the celebrated "Crossroads of the World," or, as the public relations pioneer Edward Bernays boasted back in 1918, "the center of the universe."

If the crossroads slogan was, in fact, a bit of brilliantly deployed public relations hyperbole, Times Square has more than lived up to the claim.

shaped Times Square with their theaters, dance halls, and restaurants, had a decidedly more zealous mission: to create the greatest entertainment zone the world had ever known, and by logical extension the most freewheeling district that contemporary mores would allow.

Times Square's style was born in a pleasure and profit milieu amid an unlikely confluence of Wild West, effete European, and crass New York aesthetic influences. The music halls, roof gardens, nightclubs, and even flea circuses fused into a hybrid of rough and ready Tenderloin and pop culture Rialto districts. This new being challenged the proprieties of the entrenched upper-crust New Yorkers who protested in countless magazine and newspaper articles what they believed was the irreparable debasement of their cultural bedrock. They despised the Flo Ziegfelds, Irving Berlins, and other famous Times Square impresarios as defilers of high art and injected a sinister anti-semitism into their critiques. Yet they were right to be threatened; the accused despoilers ultimately prevailed, and their Times Square style quickly captured mass taste and conquered New York.

Times Square's style was not just rooted in a mélange of garish architecture and debatable amusements. It was also driven by the amazing march of technological progress. Innovative electric commercial signs covered buildings like vines. Many moved to rhythmic cadences and formed animated pictures and tableaux, in and of themselves a new type of entertainment spectacle that hypnotized and transfixed. Of course, the ribbon-cutting of the new Times Square subway station on October 27, 1904 (as a major investor in the neighborhood, *New York Times* publisher Adolph S. Ochs insisted the station be so named for his paper) further encouraged new pleasure seekers, which begat the need for more novel culture.

DISNEY HATTER
Broadway and 42nd Street
Silk Top Hat
C.1917

Times Square Tower building, the last of the four gigantic office towers on 42nd Street that have reshaped the area's public persona—finally opened its doors. Yet no amount of civic or political pressure to make Times Square into a corporate park or commercial mall can take the freak show entirely out of the square. Despite attempts to sanitize, corporatize, and otherwise transform the district into a destination for the whole family, strict zoning laws preserve certain aspects of Times Square's history. Sure, the porn palaces and peep shows were shunted off to less obtrusive venues, but they were only a minor blip in Times Square's overall history anyway, and barely indicative of the nostalgic style celebrated in this book.

Some of the indigenous Times Square population was indeed sordid—brothels were almost as common as brownstones and often one and the

We have now reached the centennial of the New York City subway, the Times Tower, and thus Times Square itself. The building that stands on its original footprint, One Times Square, was thoroughly rebuilt decades ago. Today it is an empty shell, more profitable for hanging advertising scrims, animated news zippers, and LED screens than housing tenants. The centennial also comes as the year in which the final jewel in the crown of Times Square's massive refurbishing—the same—yet through the gauze of time and, more importantly, the virtuosity of Damon Runyon's colorful character sketches, today those denizens appear as veritable saints compared to the more recent transient population. Although Runyonesque dwellers prowled the streets, worked the brothels, ran the numbers, and read their racing forms in dingy hot dog dispensaries, they were transformed for the reader and voyeur into dramatic characters with comic monikers who spoke evocative slang. There were hustlers, con artists, and derelicts to be sure, but today they occupy a nostalgic corner in the collective memory of Times Square. Although this may be a romanticized version of reality, even romance and myth are rooted in fact—after all, Runyon was a journalist. Times Square may sometimes be portrayed as a colorful *Guys and Dolls* theater set, but a more accurate depiction comes in the gritty noir film *Sweet Smell of Success*. Plays and movies notwith-standing, the real Times Square has always been stranger (and more magnificent) than any of the fiction it has inspired.

Even in the mid-1960s, during its slide into disrepute, many of the grand old buildings, theaters, and "spectaculars" (a term coined by Douglas Leigh, creator of many of Times Square's most ambitious advertising displays) that exemplified the square's epic past were still standing—albeit on their last legs. The most imposing landmarks were the Astor Hotel (now replaced by the Viacom Building), the lavish Roxy Theater, the legendary Paramount Theater (the exterior of which is currently reconstituted with a new digital marquee), and the historic Camels Cigarette billboard on the old Claridge Hotel (where the American Broadcasting Company now has a fishbowl studio). When World War II forced nightly blackouts, Leigh designed the smoking component to avoid using lights. For almost thirty years, this

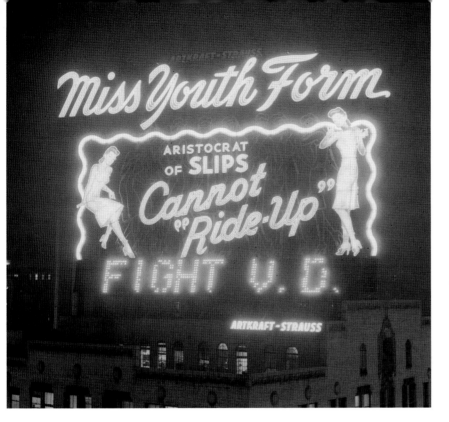

MISS YOUTH FORUM
This spectacular was used in the
fight against veneral disease.
Electric Sign
1948

Nearby, foam ceaselessly bubbled over a humongous blue bottle of Bromo Seltzer. And then there was the A&P Coffee cup, which emptied and refilled itself every fifteen minutes, and which originally released the scent of fresh coffee into the street. (This had to be stopped during World War II because coffee was rationed and the smell drove pedestrians crazy.) Another emblem was the famous electric zipper wrapping around the old Times Building, which before commercial radio provided "hot off the wire" news to thousands of New Yorkers. And let's not forget the walk-in gems, like the classic Horn and Hardart automat or the fluorescent-lit, vest-pocket Nedicks hot dog and orange drink stands that satisfied Times Square's mass appetites.

emblematic advertising spectacle blew smoke rings over Broadway's passersby until surrendering to the cancer of urban blight in the mid-1970s.

There were other doomed but remembered landmarks that defined Times Square. Pepsi-Cola's cascading waterfall, which continuously recycled 50,000 gallons of water per minute, was a monument to advertising ingenuity atop the Bond clothing store (now Toys R Us). It was designed to compete with Coca-Cola's massive bull's-eye neon sign over Duffy Square. The Kool Cigarette penguin stood atop a giant cake of ice, winking one hundred thousand times a day.

Less monumental, though no less consequential, are the forgotten Times Square artifacts in this book. Designed to publicize the attractions of Times Square at home and abroad, a distinct graphic style combining commercial vernaculars and quirky mannerisms took hold. Produced by anonymous printers, sign painters, and graphic designers, the archetype of Times Square's visual language was more carnival than urbane, yet it built upon a cosmopolitan sensibility. Graphics helped define the various sectors of Times Square: theater programs used Victorian, art nouveau, and art deco ornamental motifs as fashion demanded; Tin Pan Alley song sheets were emblazoned with chic patterns that changed with the hemlines; ritzy restaurants used flapper and streamline conceits as long as they were modish; hotels promoted their grandeur with showy images and pseudo-elegant typographies. In addition to hi-tone stylistic mannerisms, common commercial-art tropes—bold gothic and feminine script typefaces, simplified linear stock illustrations, vivid

publicity photos—were reflexively attached to a wide range of advertisements, flyers, programs, and other sorts of printed material. Moreover, the Times Square name was used to "brand" various products: tobacco, beverages, apparel, cosmetics—any consumable that might profitably benefit from such an association.

Times Square's graphic style was ostensibly contemporary, though not modern in an avant-garde sense. International styles like art nouveau and art deco were utilized because the populace could easily identify with them, and printers had the templates on hand. Radical approaches like the Bauhaus method were rejected as too ascetic for the carnival ethos. From its nascence, when the electric sign-making innovator O. J. Gude reportedly dubbed Broadway "The Great White Way," advertising spectacles employed the most up-to-date technologies and imaginative artisans. But as the goal of such displays was commercial, the

MR. MILLER OF
THE TIMES
The story of a reporter in
the center of the world.
Book Cover
1931

The title *Times Square Style* suggests a movement or fashion that was part and parcel of a predetermined branding strategy. Nothing can be further from the truth. Like the old Times Square itself, the graphics seen here are a collision of disparate mannerisms fusing into an alternately stylized and tawdry mass of type, image, and color. If viewed through the lens of graphic design history, these artifacts defy pigeonholing. Indeed, they constitute a chaotic mess of tropes and mannerisms. But when seen as representative of Times Square's outlandish history, these lost objects underscore the eccentric spirit of an extraordinary place, the epicenter of both the highest and lowest culture New York City has to offer.

resulting look was determined by what would best stimulate mass consumption. Electric signs were inherently gaudy (although often conceptually clever); printed and painted billboards were dramatically overt; posted and pasted bills were graphically bold. Logos, trademarks, trade characters, and brand names were the meat of Times Square graphics. Advertising agencies simply tried to get messages out; making headway in the progress of design theory and practice was of no real consequence.

While other great cities may lay claim to the crossroads mantle, New York's Times Square is the genuine article. Once the city emerged in the late nineteenth century as the marketplace of the nation—the Northeast's principal commercial port and, thanks to Grand Central Station, a major railroad terminus—it was ordained that some pivotal locale would *of the* become a magnet for visitors and natives alike. Certain patricians would have preferred somewhere closer to the city's downtown heart, but once August Belmont's Independent Rapid Transit Corporation (IRT) laid its tracks beyond midtown, the great divide between the old and the new New York was breached. In 1904, the same year that the subway station opened at 42nd Street, construction was completed on publisher Adolph Ochs's stately Times Tower at the center of the hub then known as Longacre Square. Ochs further persuaded Mayor George McClellan to rename the junction, where William H. Vanderbilt had once directed the city's horse-trading exchange, to Times Square.

Soon enough, the name became a synonym for spectacle. But the original impetus for this entertainment carnival had already been in place for almost a decade. In 1895, after much delay, impresario Oscar Hammerstein I had opened his block-long Olympia Theater, which he called "the grandest amusement temple in the world." This mammoth and ornate structure featured three theaters and a magnificent roof garden on a scale that was unprecedented in the city. In addition, Hammerstein constructed two other majestic theaters and the glass- enclosed Paradise Roof Garden, which housed exotic birds and domesticated monkeys (something of a metaphor for Times Square itself). His intermingling of high and low produced a uniquely American popular art. Between 1904 and 1917 Times Square was a tabula rasa; boosted by aggressive public relations and grand visionaries, it became a showcase of lustrous culture and commerce that merged, like Broadway and Seventh Avenue, into the most vibrant commercial crossroads of the world.

CROSSROADS of the WORLD

[PREVIOUS PAGE]
VJ DAY

A signature image from
a special day in Times Square.

Photograph by Lt. Victor Jorgensen
AUGUST 14, 1945

[OPPOSITE]
D-DAY

Crowds watch the news zipper on the
New York Times building.

*Photograph by Howard Hollem,
Edward Meyers*
JUNE 6, 1944

C.1917

C.1908

THE NEW YORK TIMES BUILDING
Three views of the cathedral of the Square.

Postcards

C.1910

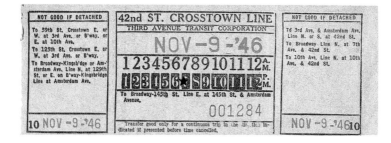

42ND STREET CROSSTOWN

Bus Transfer
1946

IWO JIMA

50-foot statue of Marines raising the
flag at The 7th War Loan rally.
MAY 12, 1945

5TH WAR LOAN

This giant cash register recorded
the sales of war bonds.
JUNE 13, 1944

[OPPOSITE]

LIBERTY

A facsimile of the Statue of Liberty looks on as
crowds celebrate Germany's surrender.

MAY 7, 1945

[ABOVE]

TIMES SUBWAY STATION

Opening day of the first Times Square
and 42nd Street subway station.

Photograph by Robert L. Bracklow

OCTOBER 27, 1904

[ABOVE]

U.S. MAIL

Night club entertainer Ted Lewis and friends buy stamps
at a giant mail box across from the Hotel Claridge.

Photograph by Phyllis Twachtman

1961

[OPPOSITE]

HAPPY NEW YEAR

Seen from atop the Times
building, crowds assemble to
celebrate in the Square.

1937

That Times Square has so many evocative nicknames is indicative of its station as a multipurpose cultural and commercial center. But when the lighting display entrepreneur O. J. Gude initially coined the enduring moniker "The Great White Way," he was really more intent on promoting the unprecedented outdoor luminescent advertisements his company was constructing up and down Broadway. With its pleasing ring, it also turned into a hook that captured the public's imagination, enticing people into the area from all over the nation and the world. Indeed, this promotional slogan also became synonymous with Times Square's other famous asset—the scores of legitimate and illegitimate theaters whose marquees were perpetually aglow with static and modulating incandescent light. Broadway, the center of American theater, has always been the place where actors and actresses want so desperately to "see their name in lights." In addition to this artificial wattage, performers find it desirable to be on the cover of the theater programs and show biz magazines that have papered the area for so long. From the outset, Broadway's graphics were dressed in a style designed to celebrate notoriety. Influenced both by the legendary lights and the ornamental conceits of the day—from art nouveau to art deco—it was visual hyperbole in the most dramatic manner. When a leading man or woman's portrait was not available, printers and commercial artists worked with stock or stylized illustrations, often romantic in tenor, that evoked a musical or dramatic essence. Others were tastefully decorative. Among the common stereotypes were women playing lyres, men dressed as jesters, Greek drama masks, and ethereal dancers galore. Often the grandiose theaters themselves were the graphic stars; grand marquees with illuminated names set in stark and elegant typefaces were the most important attractions on Broadway.

The GREAT WHITE WAY

VANDERBILT THEATRE

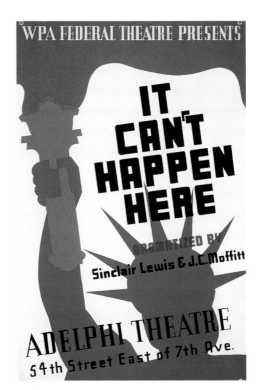

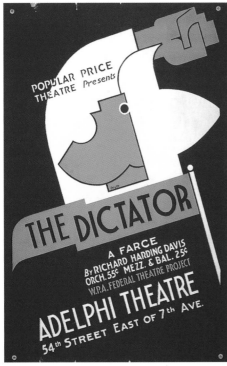

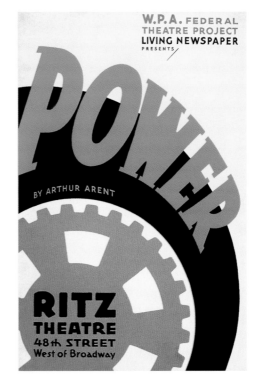

THE GHETTO

Advertising for Broadway shows
came in all styles and colors.

Poster
1899

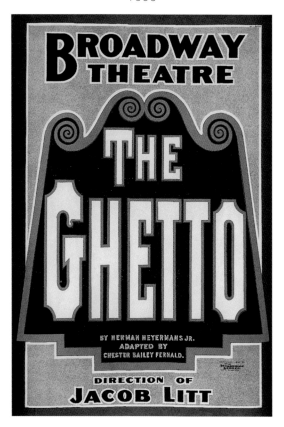

[OPPOSITE]

WPA

The Federal Theatre Project (1935–39) was the first and only
government-sponsored theater program in United States history.

SING FOR YOUR SUPPER

Poster by Aida McKenzie
1939

THE DICTATOR

Poster By Herbert Pratt
C. 1938

IT CAN'T HAPPEN HERE

Poster
1936

POWER

Poster
1937

42ND STREET

One of the most remembered films to capture the
Broadway theatre on the silver screen.
1933

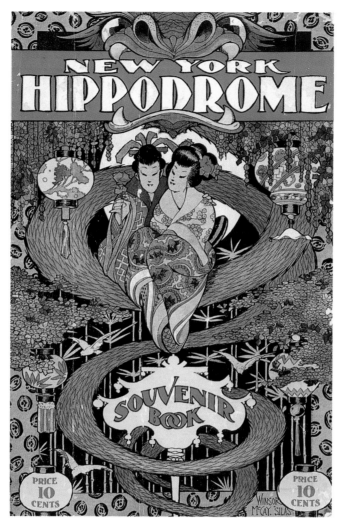

Souvenir Book
1 9 0 9

NEW YORK HIPPODROME THEATRE

The New York Hippodrome Theatre, known in 1909 as the largest playhouse in the world—
"The Nation's House of Wonders"—produced sumptuous spectacles that might include as
many as twelve elephants and twenty horses, and could accommodate five thousand attendees.

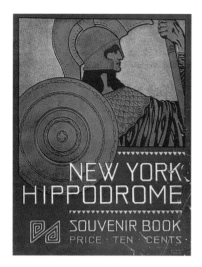

Souvenir Book
1914

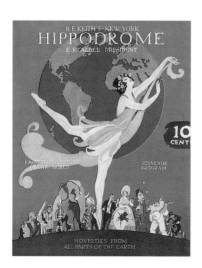

Souvenir Book
1915

Souvenir Book
1912

RADIO CITY
MUSIC HALL

SHOW PLACE OF THE NATION

PROGRAM

HAROLD K SIMON

[OPPOSITE]

PROGRAM

Designed by Harold K. Simon
1936

RADIO CITY MUSIC HALL

Just a few blocks from Times Square, Radio City had one of the largest stages
in the world, with a great proscenium arch built to resemble a sunburst.

Postcard
1940

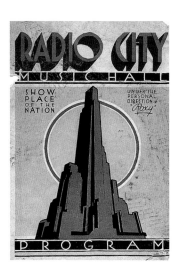

Program
1937

Program
1932

Postcard
1940

THE WINTER GARDEN

50TH ST. & BROADWAY

A MUSIC HALL DEVOTED TO THE CONTINENTAL IDEA OF VARIETE

WINTER GARDEN CO.
MANAGERS

RADIO CITY MUSIC HALL, NEW YORK CITY

ROSE OF WASHINGTON SQU

Song

Lyric by
Ballard Macdon

Music by
James F. Hanle

As Introduced by

FANNY BRI

in the new

Ziegfeld Midnight

atop the
New Amsterdam Theatr
New York.

Price 60 cents

Programme

So this is Gay Paree...
Come on along with me—
we're stepping out to see
the LATIN QUARTER

NEW YORK DRAMATIC NEWS

APRIL 17, 1915.   PRICE TEN CENTS

OSCAR HAMMERSTEIN

NEW YORK CITY

CITY

After the Theatre at the Knickerbocker

THEATRE GUILD

MAGAZINE

THE NAPOLEON OF BROADWAY

The Amazing Story of the Late
Joe Leblang, Merchant Prince and
Capitalist of the New York Theatre

BY HOWARD BARNES

• 25 CENTS •

MAY · 1931

McBRIDE'S

THEATRE TICKET OFFICE
INC.

MAIN OFFICES

UPTOWN
1493 BROADWAY—LAckawanna 4-3900

DOWNTOWN
71 BROADWAY—BOwling Green 9-6600

LONDON
KEITH PROWSE Ltd.
90 NEW BOND ST.

AMUSEMENTS IN NEW

ALVIN   52nd Street, West of Broadway
"NO TIME FOR SERGEANTS" (Comedy)
Daily 8.30   Also Wed. and Sat. 2.30

BARRYMORE   47th Street, West of Broadway
Wednesday Evening, October 26, 1955
GLADYS COOPER—SIOBHAN McKENNA In
"THE CHALK GARDEN" (Drama)
Daily 8.40   Also Saturday 2.40

BECK   45th Street, at 8th Avenue
ELI WALLACH and JOHN BEAL In
"THE TEAHOUSE OF THE AUGUST MOON" (Comedy)
Daily 8.40   Also Wed. and Sat. 2.40

BELASCO   44th Street, East of Broadway
"WILL SUCCESS SPOIL ROCK HUNTER?" (Comedy)
Daily 8.40   Also Wed. and Sat. 2.40

BIJOU   45th Street, West of Broadway
JOYCE GRENFELL Requests The Pleasure (Revue)
Daily 8.30   Also Wed. and Sat. 2.30
Sunday Eve., Oct 30th—Benefit Performance
In Aid of The Actors' Fund

BROADHURST   44th Street, West of Broadway
SHIRLEY BOOTH In
"THE DESK SET" (Comedy)
Daily 8.40   Also Wed. and Sat. 2.40

BROADWAY   Broadway and 53rd Street
Tuesday Evening, October 25, 1955
COMEDIE FRANCAISE
"LE BOURGEOIS GENTILHOMME"
Tues to Sun. 8.30   Also Sat. and Sun. 2.30

CARNEGIE HA
Tues. Eve.
Wed. Eve.
Thurs. Eve.
Fri. Aft. ....
Fri. Eve. ....
Sat. Morn.
Sat. Eve. ...
Sun. Aft. ..
Sun. Eve. ..

CITY CENTER
Wed. to Sun

CORONET
"A VIEW
Daily 8.30

CORT
JO
"THE DIA
Daily 8.40

FORTY-SIXTH
"DAMN
Daily 8.30

GOLDEN
Daily 8.40

HELLINGER
ANTONIO A
Tues. to Sun

HOLIDAY
Thursda
J
"D
Daily 8.40

McBRIDE'S—Downtown, 71 B'way,

7th Ave. and 57th St.

HARMONIA OF LONDON
HARMONIA OF LONDON
LHARMONIC-SYMPHONY
LHARMONIC-SYMPHONY
HARMONIA OF LONDON
UNG PEOPLE'S CONCERT
EVENING IN OLD RUSSIA
LHARMONIC-SYMPHONY
..........................ESCUDERO

130 West 56th Street

Y OPERA
Also Sat. and Sun. 2.30

h Street, West of Broadway

LIN In
BRIDGE" (Drama)
Also Wed. and Sat. 2.30

th Street, East of Broadway

DKRAUT In
E FRANK" (Drama)
Also Wed. and Sat. 2.40

46th St., West of Broadway

RDON In
(Musical Comedy)
Also Wed. and Sat. 2.30

h Street, West of Broadway

BORGE
N MUSIC"
Also Wed. and Sat. 2.40

st Street, West of Broadway

H BALLET COMPANY
Also Sat. and Sun. 2.30

Broadway and 47th Street

October 27, 1955
JOHN
ELAND In
(Melodrama)
Also Saturday 2.40

IMPERIAL   45th Street, West of Broadway
HILDEGARDE   DON
NEFF   AMECHE In
"SILK STOCKINGS" (Musical Comedy)
Daily 8.30   Also Wed. and Sat. 2.30

LONGACRE   48th Street, West of Broadway
"THE YOUNG AND BEAUTIFUL" (Comedy)
Daily 8.30   Also Wed. and Sat. 2.30

LYCEUM   45th Street, East of Broadway
MAURICE CHEVALIER
Daily (Incl. Sun.) 8.40   Also Saturday 2.40
Sunday Eve., Nov. 6th—Benefit Performance
In Aid of The Actors' Fund

MAJESTIC   44th Street, West of Broadway
EZIO PINZA—WALTER SLEZAK In
"FANNY" (Musical Play)
Daily 8.25   Also Wed. and Sat. 2.25

MILLER'S   43rd Street, East of Broadway
"WITNESS FOR THE PROSECUTION" (Mystery)
Daily 8.40   Also Thurs. and Sat. 2.40

MOROSCO   45th Street, West of Broadway
BARBARA BEL GEDDES—BURL IVES In
"CAT ON A HOT TIN ROOF" (Drama)
Daily 8.30   Also Wed. and Sat. 2.30

MUSIC BOX   45th Street, West of Broadway
"BUS STOP" (Comedy)
Daily 8.30   Also Thurs. and Sat. 2.30

NATIONAL   41st Street, West of Broadway
MELVYN DOUGLAS In
"INHERIT THE WIND" (Drama)
Daily 8.30   Also Wed. and Sat. 2.30

PLAYHOUSE   48th Street, East of Broad
PATRICIA NEAL In
"A ROOMFUL OF ROSES" (Comedy)
Daily 8.40   Also Wed. and Sat. 2

PLYMOUTH   45th Street, West of Broad
MICHAEL REDGRAVE In
"TIGER AT THE GATES" (Drama)
Daily 8.40   Also Wed. and Sat. 2

ROYALE   45th Street, West of Broad
"THE BOY FRIEND" (Musical Comedy)
Daily 8.45   Also Wed. and Sat. 2

ST. JAMES   44th Street, West of Broad
JOHN   EDDIE   HELEN
RAITT   FOY, JR. GALLAGHER In
"THE PAJAMA GAME" (Musical Comedy)
Daily 8.30   Also Wed. and Sat. 2

SHUBERT   44th Street, West of Broad
D'OYLY CARTE OPERA COMPANY
Monday, Tuesday, Wednesday Eves., Wednesday M
"IOLANTHE"
Thursday, Friday, Saturday Eves., Saturday Mat.
"THE PIRATES OF PENZANCE"
Daily 8.30   Also Wed. and Sat. 2

WINTER GARDEN   Broadway and 50th Str
"PLAIN AND FANCY" (Musical Comedy)
Daily 8.30   Also Wed. and Sat. 2

SUNDAY PERFORMANCES

ACTOR'S PLAYHOUSE ......Out Of This World (M &
BECK ....The Teahouse Of The August Moon (Oct. 23
BIJOU ....Joyce Grenfell (Oct. 30
BROADWAY ....Comedie Francaise (M &
CIRCLE IN THE SQUARE ....La Ronde (M &
CITY CENTER ....Opera (M &
4TH STREET ....The Cherry Orchard (M &
HELLINGER ....Antonio (M &
JAN HUS AUDITORIUM ....Macbeth
LYCEUM ....Maurice Chevalier
PHOENIX ....The Carefree Tree (M &
THEATRE DE LYS ......The Threepenny Opera (M &
YIDDISH ART ....The Shepherd King (M &

MCBRIDE'S

The famous theater ticket office was located
next to the Paramount Theatre.

Schedule
1955

THE PLAYBILL®

The long running journal of Broadway
has been a mainstay since the twenties.

C. 1938

BALCONY & ORCHESTRA

The basic design of the Broadway
ticket has not changed much in
sixty years, but the price has.

Theatre Ticket Stubs
1947–58

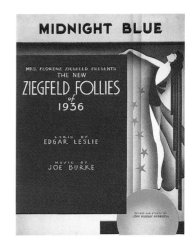

ZIEGFELD FOLLIES

Florenz Ziegfeld's fabled Follies was the most lavish and modern attraction on Broadway. The Zeigfeld Theater and sets were designed by Joseph Urban, the modernist architect, in a heroic moderne style. For every new annual Follies, song sheets, posters, and programs were specially produced.

Song Sheets
1908 – 36

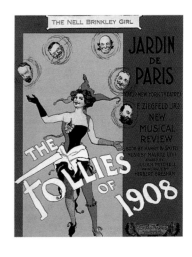

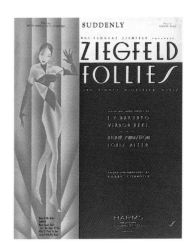

M-G-M'S ZIEGFELD FOLLIES

When movies became popular, the Follies
was a prime source of material.

Movie Poster
1946

[RIGHT]

M'LLE ANNA HELD'S EYES

Anna Held was Flo Ziegfeld's first wife and muse.
This poster is an example of how Ziegfeld promoted
her expressive eyes, which were heralded in her
signature song, "I Can't Make My Eyes Behave."

Theatrical Poster
C.1898

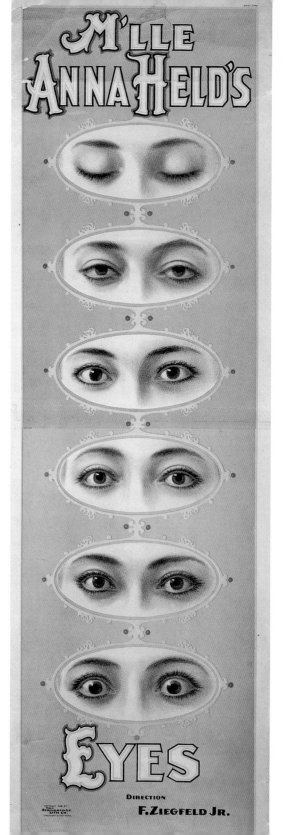

Programs were designed as much to commemorate the theaters as the shows. These (and those on pages 44–7) are lavish evocations of the grandeur of the Broadway theater.

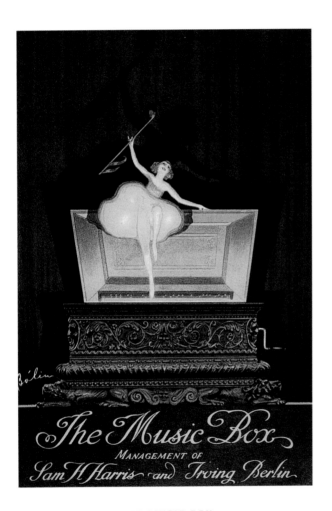

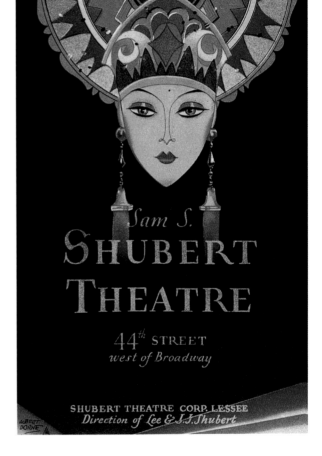

THE MUSIC BOX

Theater Program
Designed by Bólin
1930

SAM S. SHUBERT THEATRE

Theater Program
Designed by Albert Dorne
1930

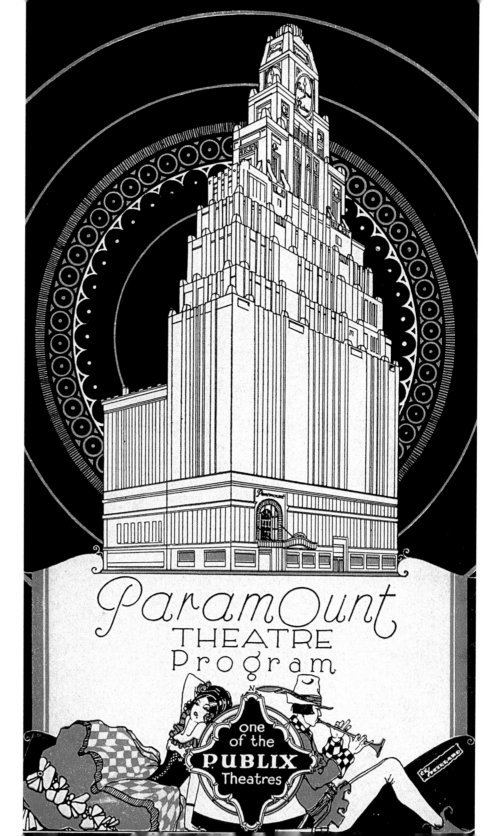

PARAMOUNT
THEATRE
Movie Program
1927

Theater Program
1916

Theater Program
1921

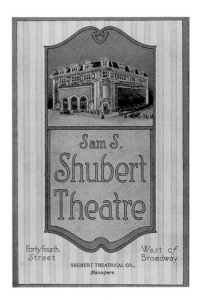

Theater Program
1916

Theater Program
Designed by F. Earl Christy
1 9 2 1

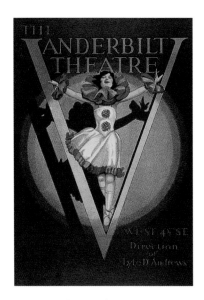

Theater Program
1 9 2 9

Theater Program
1 9 1 6

1908

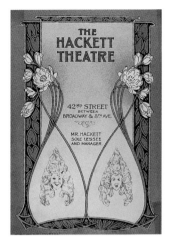

1909

1912–13

1913

1915

1916

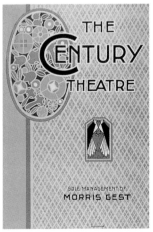

1919

1920

1921

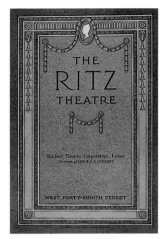

1925

1926

1927

1927

1927

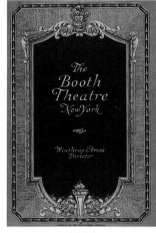

1928

1928

1929

1930

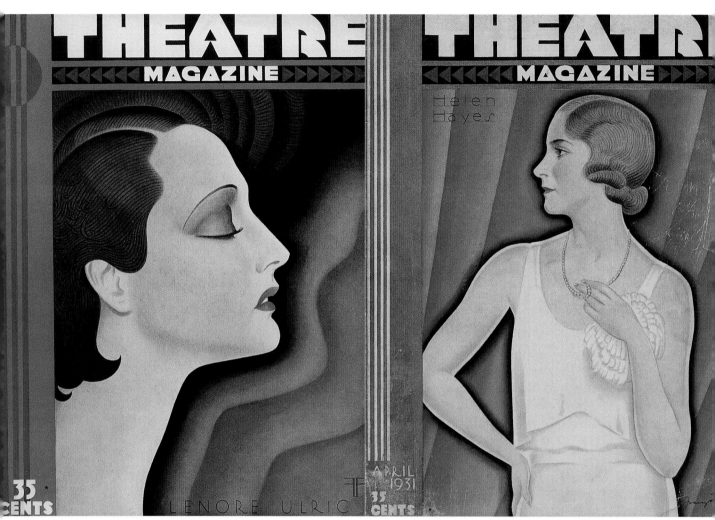

THEATRE MAGAZINE

This magazine, the clarion of the legitimate theater, was designed in the art deco style to convey
the exotic elegance of the art. Every issue was devoted to a particular Broadway star.

Magazine Covers
Illustrations by Franz Felix

JANUARY 1917

MAY 1917

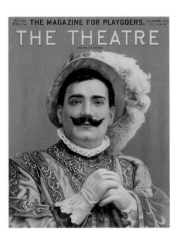

DATE UNKNOWN

JANUARY 1918

THEATRE MAGAZINE

In its earlier incarnation, the magazine covers were highly stylized, hand-colored photographs of leading performers in their costumes. The portraits were photographed by Ira L. Hill Studio and Aime Dupont.

Magazine Covers

FEBRUARY 1924

MAY 1924

APRIL 1924

JANUARY 1924

THEATRE MAGAZINE

Some covers were less about the individual stars than
the roles that they popularized at the time. Baskerville
illustrated these in a lavish and idealized manner.

Magazine Covers
Illustrated by Baskerville

By the 1920s, carnival midway attractions shared center stage with legitimate theaters. While the Cole Brothers Circus played the Hippodrome, Harry Houdini performed on Broadway and lesser entertainments filled 42nd Street. Prohibition put grandiose dining establishments like Murray's Roman Gardens out of business. In their place, Hubert's Museum and Flea Circus offered a somewhat less sophisticated clientele a nightly diet of "flying fleas," Ajax the Sword Swallower, Ibera the "double bodied individual," Albert-Alberta the half-man/half-woman, and Waldo, who swallowed live mice onstage. In 1939, Ripley's three-story Odditorium extended the freak show tradition with the world's only living two-headed baby, "imported from Sumatra." But the most popular attraction was burlesque. (The word is taken from the Italian word *burla*, meaning "jest.") Burley shows came to Times Square after vaudeville started its decline, and took over many of the darkened old theaters. The Minsky family had become synonymous with burlesque beginning in its earliest days,

and was responsible for developing and perfecting the format. Their shows combined comedy sketches (their comedians included Fanny Brice, Abbott and Costello, and Bert Lahr), scantily clad chorus-line dancers and, of course, strippers. It was the strip tease, which dated back to the late-nineteenth century, that attracted customers away from vaudeville and the movies. During the Depression, burlesque was hugely profitable. While Gypsy Rose Lee and Sally Rand introduced an "artistic" twist to "exotic dancing," most strip shows were quite bawdy, contributing to Times Square's growing unsavory reputation. Crackdowns half-heartedly began during the mid-1920s, but in 1939 Mayor Fiorello LaGuardia led an aggressive morality charge from the back of a fire truck. One by one he padlocked the burlesque theaters, strip joints, and houses of prostitution along 42nd Street. This cleansed the neighborhood for a while, but eventually adult movie theaters established a beachhead in old Times Square, and the place became more lurid than ever.

HONKY TONK *Boulevard*

[ABOVE]

HUBERT'S MUSEUM

The tattooed lady (top), sword swallower (right), and tall man (left) were among the sideshow acts performing at Hubert's Museum on West 42nd Street in what had once been Murray's Roman Gardens.

C.1930

[OPPOSITE]

THE ELTINGE THEATER

Named for famed female impersonator Julian Eltinge, this theater opened in 1912 on West 42nd Street as a legitimate house, but in 1931 turned to burlesque. Later it became the Empire Theater.

C.1931

BILLY ROSE'S DIAMOND HORSESHOE

Night Club Program
C . 1 9 4 4

HIGH AND LOW

Times Square was alive with freak shows and strip teases that gave it a unique yet shady character. Some of the attractions were. . .

MINSKY'S ORIENTAL THEATRE

Theater Pass
C. 1936

RIPLEY'S ODDITORIUM

Postcard
1939

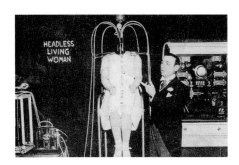

RIPLEY'S ODDITORIUM

Postcard
1939

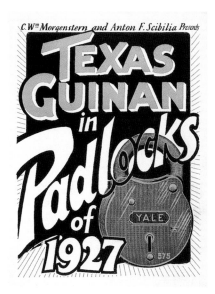

PADLOCKS OF 1927

Theater Flyer
1927

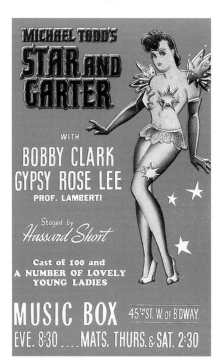

STAR & GARTER

Theatrical Flyer
C. 1938

[OPPOSITE]

RIPLEY'S ODDITORIUM

Three stories of the most amazing and absurd
attractions ever presented in New York.
Postcard
1 9 3 9

PROFESSOR HECKLER'S FLEA CIRCUS

Hubert's Museum was known for its novel
circus, in which the tiny creatures flew around
a contraption made from toothpicks.
C . 1 9 3 5

C.1930.

C.1932

THE CIRCUS

Billy Rose and the Cole Brothers were among the acts who brought wild
animals and wild music (including the Paul Whitman orchestra) to Times
Square. The most popular of all was Charlie Weir's Baby Elephants.

Posters and Advertisements

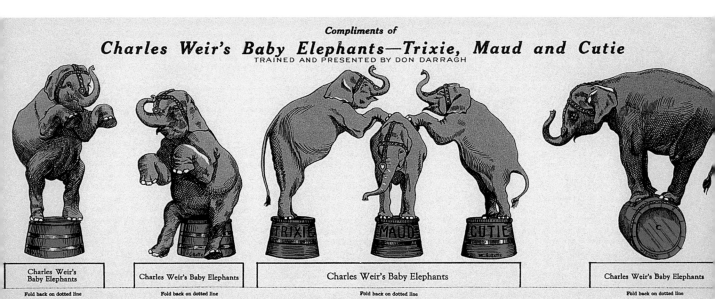

C.1930

HOUDINI & COMPANY

The great illusionists flocked to play Times Square, among them the great mesmerizer Kellar, his successor, Thurston, and the incomparable escape artist, Harry Houdini.

Posters

1917

GEORGE WHITE'S SCANDALS

There were few more enticing words for a Broadway show than "scandal." Mostly they were musical varieties that featured real headliners, rather than tawdry strippers, but with a touch of the wicked as accent.

Lobby Card
1935

Song Sheet
1934

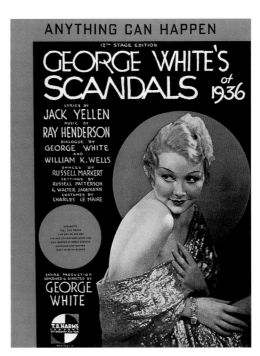

Song Sheet
1929

Song Sheet
1936

Song Sheet
1939

The popular musical bazaar located in Times Square, known to sheet music consumers the world over as Tin Pan Alley, earned its euphonious moniker when it was first located on 28th Street between Broadway and Sixth Avenue. (The din of pianists demonstrating their songs wafted from open windows to the street below, forming the eponymous chorus of "clashing tin pans.") During the early 1910s, Manhattan's hit factories moved to Times Square, where for follow-ing generations they were head-quartered in the legendary Brill Building at 1619 Broadway. Al-though the appellation was affixed to the overall popular music "industry," everyone knew that there was only one real Tin Pan Alley, and it became a mecca for composers and lyri-cists looking to strike it rich. The veritable king of this block was young Irving Berlin, who composed more hits and launched more musical crazes than any other pop composer. The rise of Tin Pan Alley owed a debt to the unprecedented surge in demand for the travelling shows that toured the nation. Fol-lowing the Broadway variety archetype, booking agents from New York regularly dispatched variety acts to play on the road or on the so-called vaude-ville circuit. Before leaving New York, performers routinely stopped at Tin Pan Alley publishing offices to stock up on new songs and novel arrange-ments. Sheet music was the flat record of the gilded age, and was marketed as such to the general public through eye-catching covers that were fervently promoted in theaters, beer halls, saloons, lobster palaces, and nickelodeon movie houses. Each era in Tin Pan Alley's history had its own distinctive graphic style, from art nouveau to art deco and every mannerism in between. But soon there was a new game in town. By 1908, the gramophone and flat discs with neutral labels and sleeves began to take over. By the 1920s, records were big business. After World War II the record industry found sources of talent beyond Tin Pan Alley. No longer the hit machine it once was, Tin Pan Alley will be forever celebrated as the first cap-ital of American popular music.

BROADWAY

ELECTRICALLY RECORDED

1075-A

Fox Trot
Vocal Chorus
The Joyboys

Me and My Shadow

(Billy Rose - Al Jolson - Dave Dreyer)

Ralph Sherman's Orchestra

644

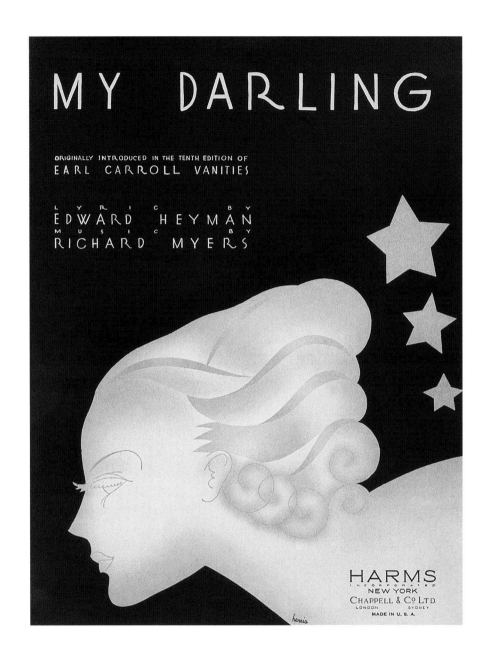

MY DARLING

Songwriters flocked to the Brill Building to find fame and
fortune with the hit that would make Americans swoon.

Song Sheet
1927

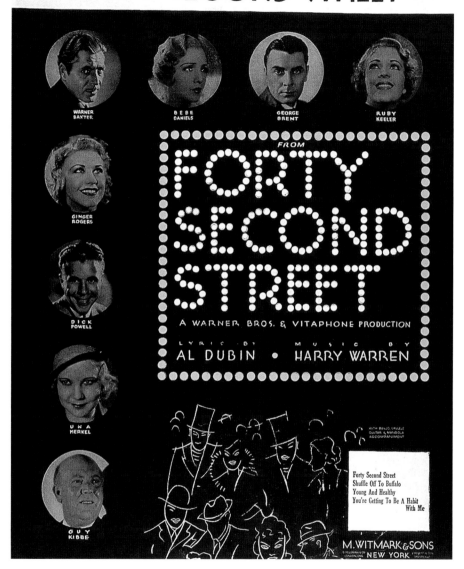

FORTY SECOND STREET

Tin Pan Alley was known for the hits it produced as song sheets. This was the age when people brought home songs to play in their parlors.

Song Sheet
1933

Song Sheet
1934

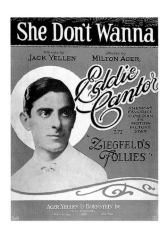

Song Sheet
C.1920

Song Sheet
1919

Song Sheet
1943

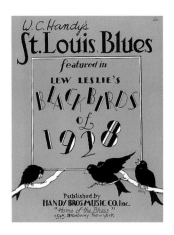

Song Sheet
1928

Song Sheet
1942

LULLABY OF BROADWAY

Irving Berlin was the biggest hit-writer on the Alley, but he was not alone
in churning out the sheets that raised the tempo of Broadway.

[OPPOSITE]

HITTIN' THE CEILING

Song Sheet
1929

HITTIN' THE CEILING

Carl Laemmle's Stupendous Talking and Singing Picture

BROADWAY

with

SONGS BY CON CONRAD, SIDNEY D. MITCHELL AND ARCHIE GOTTLER

Sing A Little Love Song
The Chicken Or The Egg
Broadway
Hittin' The Ceiling
Hot-Footin' It

from Jed Harris' greatest of all Stage Dramas
by PHILIP DUNNING and GEORGE ABBOT

A PAUL FEJOS PRODUCTION —
CARL LAEMMLE JR. Associate Producer

IT'S A UNIVERSAL

DE SYLVA, BROWN AND HENDERSON, INC.
Music Publishers
DeSylva Brown & Henderson Building   745 Seventh Ave., New York

FORTY-FIVE MINUTES FROM BROADWAY

SONG SUCCESSES FROM
GEO. M COHAN'S
LATEST MUSICAL PLAY
PLAYED BY
FAY TEMPLETON
UNDER THE DIRECTION OF
KLAW & ERLANGER

FORTY-FIVE MINUTES FROM BROADWAY

SONGS of the PLAY
1. RETIRING FROM THE STAGE
2. I WANT TO BE A POPULAR MILLIONAIRE
3. MARY'S A GRAND OLD NAME
4. FORTY-FIVE MINUTES FROM BROADWAY
5. STAND UP AND FIGHT LIKE HELL
6. SO LONG MARY

PUBLISHED BY F. A. MILLS. 48 WEST 29TH ST., NEW YORK,

TONY LANE AND THE AIRLANE TRIO
Appearing in the
HOTEL DIXIE PLANTATION BAR AND LOUNGE
No Cover - - No Minimum - - No Cabaret Tax

Roseland Dancing
Broadway at 51st Street
"America's Foremost Ballroom"
New York City

OPERATIC EDITION

BROADWAY BLUES

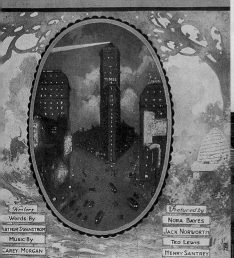

Writers
Words By
ARTHUR SWANSTROM
Music By
CAREY MORGAN

Featured by
NORA BAYES
JACK NORWORTH
TED LEWIS
HENRY SANTREY

Price 60¢

Irving Berlin, Inc.
Music Publishers
1607 Broadway

Now Open!
THE FAD OF SMART NEW YORKERS
TWO-THIRTY CLUB
MATINEE TEA DANCES
Every afternoon 2:30 to 6:00 P.M.
A most delightful way to spend an afternoon amidst pleasant surroundings
Admission $1.00 including Tea Service
(no other charges)

WORLD'S SERIES
Every game will be broadcast, play by play, thru Roseland's Radio amplifyers.

200 Hostesses
25 Hosts
in Constant
Attendance

Roseland
DANCING
Broadway at 51st Street
"America's Foremost Ballroom"
Continuous Dancing Every Afternoon & Evening

Roseland
DANCING
Broadway at 51st Street
"America's Foremost Ballroom"
New York City

AMERICA'S GREATEST REVUE
EARL CARROLL
VANITIES
TENTH EDITION
FEATURING
THE MOST BEAUTIFUL GIRLS IN THE WORLD

DIALOGUE BY
JACK McGOWAN
AND STAGED BY
EDGAR J. McGREGOR

DANCES STAGED BY
NED McGURN

SCENERY & COSTUMES DESIGNED BY
VINCENTE MINNELLI

MUSIC AND LYRICS MOSTLY BY
TED KOEHLER
AND
HAROLD ARLEN

TECHNICAL DIRECTION
W. ODEN WALLER

ALL BALLETS CREATED
AND STAGED BY
GLUCK-SANDOR

HARMS
NEW YORK
CHAPPELL & CO LTD

I Gotta Right To Sing The Blues
Along Came Love
My Darling
Take Me Away

OVER THERE

Successfully Introduced by
NORA BAYES

WILLIAM JEROME
PUBLISHING CO

Words and Music by
George M. Cohan

IT'S GREAT TO BE IN LOVE

Words and Music by CLIFF FRIEND

EARL CARROLL VANITIES

NINTH EDITION
AMERICA'S GREATEST REVUE
FEATURING THE MOST BEAUTIFUL GIRLS IN THE WORLD

ROBBINS MUSIC CORPORATION

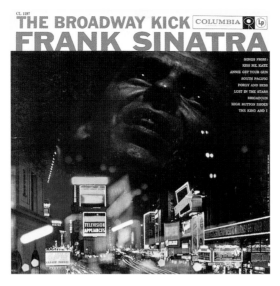

1959

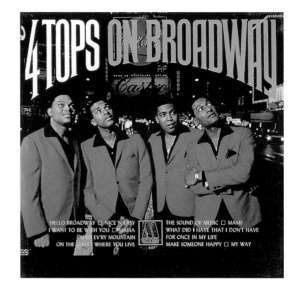

1967

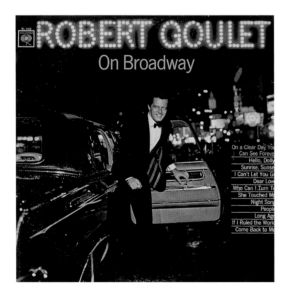

1965

1960

HIT PARADE

Broadway not only produced countless popular music hits, it was the inspiration for
many of the leading vocalists and instrumentalists during the 1950s and 1960s.

Record Albums

1967

C. 1964

1958

C. 1959

C.1960

C.1960

C.1960

C.1957

C.1960

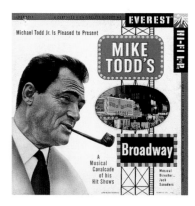

C.1958

SWINGING BROADWAY

Albums and 45s poured from the Times Square hit fountain
with covers that said "wish you were here."

Record Albums

[OPPOSITE]

LIFE IS BUT A DREAM

Times Square Records
C.1964

Times Square's attractions were designed to capture the nation's eyes and pocketbooks. Its landmark theaters, like the Theatrical Syndicate's flagship New Amsterdam (now refurbished), with its splendiferous art nouveau interior, were ornately designed to heighten the public's sense of awe, a sentiment that radiated into the hinterlands as the theater district's fabled reputation grew. But the introduction of moving pictures in 1909 forever altered the tenor of this entertainment marketplace. Hammerstein's Victoria, which provided a steady stream of vaudeville shows, began to include movies in its variety program in 1911. According to historian David C. Hammack's *Inventing Times Square*, by 1912 moviemakers were so attached to the area that they expanded their offices and built production studios to the west of Broadway. In 1915, D. W. Griffith opened his epic *Birth of A Nation* in Times Square, and its success encouraged others to use Times Square in similar fashion. The economic benefits to the motion picture industry were considerable enough to warrant major investments in grand new movie palaces, like S. L. "Roxy" Rothafel's Rialto and later the Strand, Paramount, Capitol, and Roxy—all built exclusively to exhibit films. Live theater diminished in direct relation to film's hypnotic appeal. Although Hollywood became the movie capital, movie moguls vied to have their red-carpeted premieres in Times Square's theaters. Few events were glitzier, and part of the allure was those gigantic, electrified billboards that dwarfed even the theater's blinking marquees. Movie advertisements themselves were nothing if not sensational. On an avenue known for unequalled visual vibrato, these graphics had to be the most uncompromisingly theatrical of all.

ON THE MARQUEE

THE GREAT ZIEGFELD

A big screen biography about the
greatest of Broadway impresarios.

Movie Poster
1936

CHARLIE CHAN ON BROADWAY

Mysteries played well on the seedy
Times Square streets.

Movie Poster
1937

STAGE DOOR

One of the best known Broadway
films, and with a stellar cast.

Movie Poster
1937

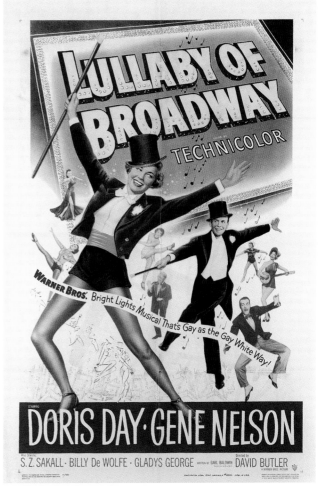

LULLABY OF BROADWAY

Tapping down the boulevard in a
film about the Great White Way.

Movie Poster
1951

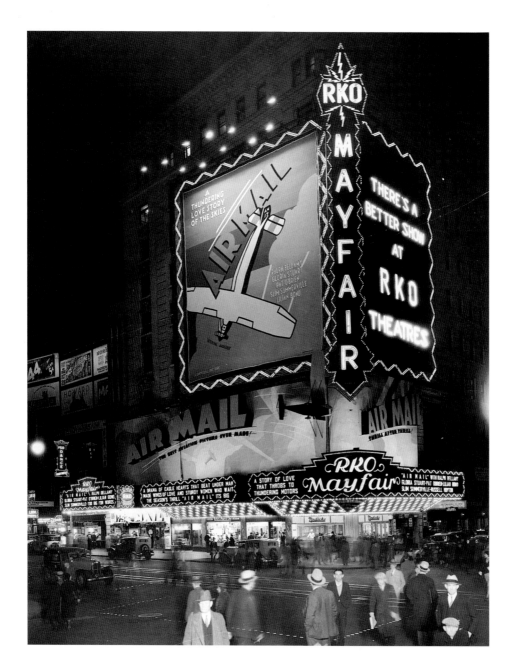

[ABOVE]

AIR MAIL

When movies hit Broadway it was with an
unprecedented electric fanfare.

Marquee and Billboard
1932

[OPPOSITE]

THE GANGSTER

Huge billboards filled the streets in the same way that
freak show posters once covered carnival midways.

Marquee and Billboard
1947

[OPPOSITE]

LOVE ME TENDER

The unveiling of the 40-foot figure of Elvis
Presley, promoting his New York City premiere
at the Paramount Theater.

Marquee
OCTOBER 28, 1956

[ABOVE]

SWEET SMELL OF SUCCESS

Burt Lancaster and Tony Curtis loom over
Broadway at the Loew's State in a movie that
told of Broadway's seamy side.

Marquee
1957

RIALTO
THE TEMPLE OF THE MOTION PICTURE

TIMES SQUARE
NEW YORK

Program Magazine

DIRECTION S.L. ROTHAPFEL

TEN
THOUSAND
GIRLS
DREAM
HER DREAM
EVERY
NIGHT

STAGE STRUCK

Technicolor THE KID SISTER FROM "PICNIC" BECOMES A STAR!

starring
HENRY FONDA · SUSAN STRASBERG
co-starring
JOAN GREENWOOD · HERBERT MARSHALL
and introducing
CHRISTOPHER PLUMMER

Screen Play by RUTH and AUGUSTUS GOETZ
WILLIAM DOZIER in Charge of Production · Produced by STUART MILLAR
Directed by SIDNEY LUMET · Music by ALEX NORTH · An RKO Radio Picture

BROADWAY RHYTHM

Dazzling with color, rhythm and song — lovely Lena Horne in the whirling
"Brazilian Boogie Woogie."

GEORGE MURPHY · GINNY SIMMS

BATTLE OF BROADWAY

with Victor McLAGLEN

Brian DONLEVY · Louise HOVICK

Raymond WALBURN · Lynn BARI · Jane DARWELL · Robert KELLARD

DAMON RUNYON'S
BLOODHOUNDS of BROADWAY
TECHNICOLOR

starring
MITZI GAYNOR · SCOTT BRADY

MITZI GREEN · MARGUERITE CHAPMAN · MICHAEL O'SHEA
WALLY VERNON · HENRY SLATE · GEORGE E. STONE · EDWIN MAX · RICHARD ALLAN

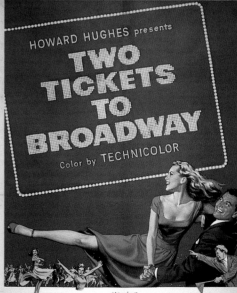

HOWARD HUGHES presents

TWO TICKETS TO BROADWAY

Color by TECHNICOLOR

starring
TONY MARTIN · JANET LEIGH
GLORIA DeHAVEN · EDDIE BRACKEN
ANN MILLER
with BARBARA LAWRENCE · BOB CROSBY featuring THE CHARLIVELS
screenplay by SID SILVERS & HAL KANTER · directed by JAMES V. KERN

GOLDEN BOY

As if in the Thanksgiving Parade, floats advertising
first run films park in front of the palatial theaters.

Display Advertisement
1939

UNDERWATER

A five-story illuminated display of Jane Russell
stood over Brandt's Mayfair Theatre.

Photograph by Herb Scharfman
1955

1936

THE GREAT ZIEGFELD

As master of Broadway, Flo Ziegfeld
and his legendary Ziegfeld Girls
were often on the movie marquee.

Posters

1941

1936

1938

1941

1944

LITTLE MISS BROADWAY, ETC.

The musicals supposedly set in Times Square had stars
like Shirley Temple, Judy Garland, and Fred Astaire
dancing up and down the boulevard.

Posters and Foyer cards

1940

1949

DUFFY SQUARE

The scene from 45th Street where
Broadway and Seventh Avenue
intersect; marquees and
advertisements clash in a panoply
of white and colored light.

1955

SIGN Spectaculars

At the turn of the century, advertising brightened the crowded boulevards of the great European cities. Commercial art in Europe relied more on enticing images than mere words. In America, advertising was focused on clever verbal slogans. Even roadside and urban billboards, the quintessential American advertising formats, were headline-heavy and without strong visuals—creatively inferior to ad work from Europe. Yet America did have a uniquely indigenous commercial aesthetic, one born of Thomas Alva Edison's incandescent revolution: the electric light display board. Paris may have been the "City of Light," but thanks to Times Square's "white light district," New York was the wellspring of technologically progressive advertising—what O. J. Gude called "The phantasmagoria of lights and electric signs." Times Square was not, in fact, the first Manhattan locale to introduce "talking signs" that telegraphed animated words and images for blocks around. But it was, in 1916, the first urban neighborhood to be officially zoned to allow such a concentrated magnitude of white and eventually colored light, not simply for illumination but to project the nation's most influential brand names to the world. By 1922, the outdoor advertising business was booming; by 1924, gasoline, soft drink, and cigarette manufacturers had taken the lion's share of available leases for major Times Square ad space. These "spectaculars," so named by Douglas Leigh, whose company conceived (and with Artkraft-Strauss, fabricated) the most inventive of the lighting displays from the late 1920s to the present day, were nothing less than high-tech carnival midway attractions. They shook, shimmied, wiggled, and blinked as they grew larger and larger. Other environmental special effects were also employed. The Times Square spectacular was semi-permanent, and the idea behind it had to really grab the public's eye. Though the masterpieces recalled here are gone—in fact, if not in memory—for the years when they were posted they served as sparkling monuments to American commercialism.

[PREVIOUS PAGE]

PEPSI-COLA

Broadway between
44th and 45th Streets
1959

SPECTACULAR SIGNS

An illuminated festival of popular American brand names defines Times Square.
The signs were as innovative as the designers who created them.

Electric Spectaculars
1914–55

ctacular sign over the PLANTERS PEANUT STORE on Broadway, New
, contains 15,000 brilliantly lighted bulbs and an animated Mr. Peanut,
gh, who magically brings various Planters Products into the magic ball.
t "PLANTERS PEANUTS" in neon flashes on and off
ous "PLANTERS PEANUTS" flow from
g at bottom of sign.

BROADWAY, A BRIGHT SPOT ALONG "THE GREAT WHITE WAY,"
SHOWING FAMOUS WRIGLEY SIGN, NEW YORK CITY   52

PEPSI-COLA

During the day the colossal billboard environment on Broadway between 44th and 45th Streets was monumental, but at night it was spectacular.

1955

RECORDED MESSAGES

Pepsi-Cola left no advertising avenue untouched.

78 RPM Record
1942

PEPSI-COLA

With his back to the illumination, Father Duffy, who was chaplain to the "Fighting 69th" Division in World War I, serves as Broadway's spiritual advisor.

Photograph by Roger Smith
C . 1 9 5 2

What do you suppose will replace the electric light?

1946

BROADWAY'S GREATEST **FREE** SHOW
...*invites sponsors in other cities*

Write or wire for
further information

DOUGLAS LEIGH INC. 630 FIFTH AVENUE
NEW YORK 20, N. Y.
CREATORS OF SPECTACULAR OUTDOOR ADVERTISING

1946

*Time takes no toll
from him who takes White Rock*

1915

LIGHTS, ACTION

Advertisements show the great
spectaculars designed by O. J. Gude
and Douglas Leigh.
C. 1915 & 1946

[OPPOSITE]

ATOP THE PALAIS D'OR

Outdoor advertisements send their
vivid messages above the marquee
of the former Palais Royal.
C. 1932

THE LAST DROP

Sign makers employed bubbling liquors and
dripping coffees to entice the public.

1941

[OPPOSITE]

CAMEL

Premium tobaccos demanded the largest signs, such
as this one, known for its persistent smoke rings.

Photograph by John Vachon

1943

[FOLLOWING PAGE]

TIMES SQUARE

Broadway and 45th Street

1936 [LEFT] & 1969 [RIGHT]

The Tower of Babel-like image on the opposite page is an apt representation of Times Square—perhaps more than the any other icon shown in this book. The palatial hotels of Times Square housed visitors from the four corners of the earth, and were designed to allow them to absorb the wonder of the towering city in the process (and of course let them soak up a little vice on the side). Depicted in printed ephemera as castles and cathedrals, Times Square's colossal hotels were as electric as any other major area attractions. For tourists it was a matter of pride to write back home on Hotel Astor letterhead or on a Royalton postcard: "Having a ball, wish you were here." Once the most sumptuous of all the hotels, the mansard-roofed Astor, centrally located between 44th and 45th streets on Broadway, offered generous accommodations that were second to none. But it was not the only magnet for the well-heeled. The Paramount, Royalton, Victoria, Taft, and Edison (the last an art-deco extravaganza) offered huge banquet halls and grand bridal suites.

ROOM WITH A VIEW

As added incentive, every room came complete with "bath, circulating ice water, and radio." With all this to boast, who would not affix a Paramount or Taft luggage label to their valise? Everyone wanted a room with a clear view of Broadway. But even if the only sight was the backside of a neighboring hotel—or worse, an airshaft—residents were within walking distance of the best view in the city and quite possibly within elevator range of one of the city's finest bars or restaurants. The Depression took the bloom off the hotel-business rose, reducing the surge of visitors to a comparative trickle. Even the swankiest establishments advertised cut-rate rooms through cheesy-looking fliers. Many of the grander establishments saw their luster erode. Times Square hotels never fully recovered from the slump, and after the war many became transient residences. Yet the era of greatness remains forever memorialized on the matchbooks, ashtrays, and other pictorial manifestations of these glorious hotels.

HOTEL TIMES SQUARE

Brochure
1939

HOTEL ASTOR

Luggage Label
1940

HOTEL PICCADILLY

Brochure
C. 1955

HOTELS ON THE SQUARE

All the leading hotels produced brochures
that extolled their virtues.

HOTEL VICTORIA

Brochure
C. 1945

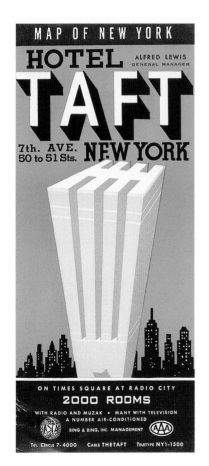

HOTEL TAFT

Brochure
C.1955

HOTEL VICTORIA

Brochure
C.1955

HOTEL TIMES SQUARE

Brochure
C.1935

FROM ASTOR TO VICTORIA

Dozens of Times Square hotels curried the
favor of visitors from all over the world. Each
offered their guests free hand-colored postcards
to send home with the hopes that they would
entice friends and relatives to visit.

Postcards and Advertisements
1920 – 55

AT THE WORLDS CROSSROADS
SHERATON-ASTOR

True New Yorkers reserve a special place in their hearts for the Sheraton-Astor Hotel. It means Times Square. Superlative dining within steps of your theatre. Glittering parties in New York's biggest ballroom. Unforgettable evenings in the Hunting Room. The Astor Bar. You'll discover a bright new look at the Astor today — where Sheraton standards are now in effect. Call the Sheraton nearest you, and make a reservation at the Sheraton-Astor soon.

SHERATON the greatest name in **HOTELS**

EXECUTIVES — Hold simultaneous meetings coast to coast via Sheraton Closed Circuit TV network. Giant screen, full color available. For brochure, write Sheraton TV, Sheraton-McAlpin Hotel, New York, N. Y.

Hotel Bristol
York City

PINK ELEPHANT BAR

PINK ELEPHANT DINING ROOM

c.1940

c.1940

c.1935

c.1939

LUGGAGE TAGS AND LABELS

Luggage labels, designed as mini coats of arms, were affixed to visitors' bags and became symbols of pride.

C. 1950

C. 1945

C. 1940

C. 1950

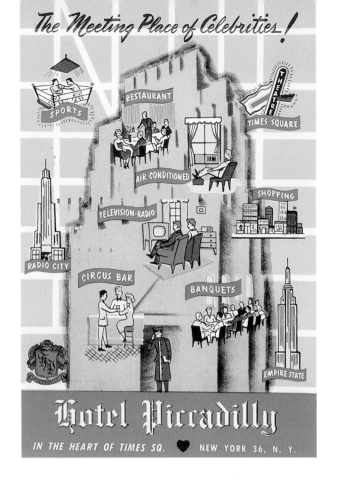

HOTEL BRISTOL

In its heyday the Bristol
was a tony redoubt.

Wine List
C. 1935

[OPPOSITE, TOP LEFT]

HOTEL PICCADILLY

This memento shows the
assets of the "Meeting
Place of Celebrities."

Postcard
C. 1955

[OPPOSITE, TOP RIGHT]

HOTEL TAFT

The Taft was one of the most
gracious hotels in the Times
Square galaxy.

Postcard
C. 1935

[OPPOSITE, BOTTOM LEFT]

HOTEL ASTOR ROOF

Swingin' bandleader Tommy
Dorsey helped give the Astor
Roof its cache.

Menu
1941

[OPPOSITE, BOTTOM RIGHT]

HOTELS TIMES SQUARE
AND BRESLIN

The 1939 New York World's
Fair was a big draw for the
city's hotels.

Souvenir Guide Book
1939

February 27, 1935

WINE LIST

HOTEL BRISTOL
129 WEST 48TH STREET.

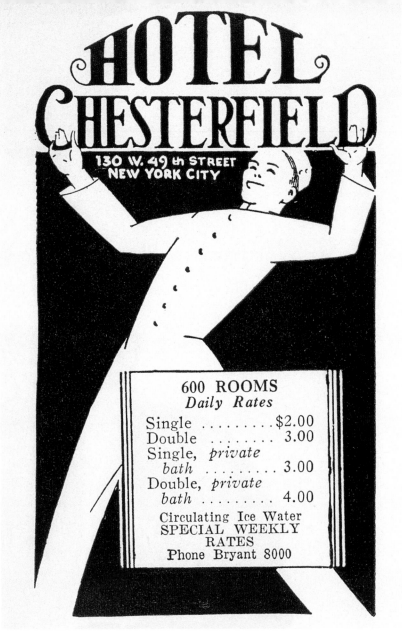

HOTEL CHESTERFIELD

After the Depression, special
hotel rates were instituted
to attract business.
Brochure
C.1931

[OPPOSITE, TOP]

HOTELS PARAMOUNT,
DIXIE, ASTOR

The gratis matchbook has been one
of the most common advertising
formats for decades.
Matchbooks
C.1935

[OPPOSITE, BOTTOM]

HOTEL TAFT

From luggage labels to ashtrays,
a hotel's logo was affixed to
anything ephemeral.
Ashtray
1932

HOTEL VICTORIA

Location was everything in
Times Square; the closer to the
attractions the better.
Business Card
C.1932

Room Key
C. 1940

HOTEL ASTOR

The key, menu, and roof garden pass all
reflect the elegance of the grand dame
of Times Square hotels before its
post-Depression decline.

Menu
C. 1950

Roof Garden Pass
1915

PLEASE DON'T DISTURB

It may not be the classiest sign,
but this Hotel Times Square door
tag gets the message across.

Room Sign
C.1950

Like all the attractions that emerged during Times Square's heyday, restaurants were designed to radiate an exaggerated aura of luxurious style that would in turn encourage free-spending extravagance from their carriage-trade patrons. Area eateries with legendary names like Rector's, Churchill's, and Murray's Roman Gardens, offered sumptuous meals in theatrical splendor served by elaborately costumed hosts and waiters. Beer gardens and oyster bars catered to the after-theater clientele. "Lobster palaces," where champagne and lobster dinners were lavishly prepared, were venues where actresses and chorus girls could meet wealthy "sporting men." Every hook was cast to attract consumers to Times Square, and soon enough new forms of entertainment were emerging. By the early teens many of the Square's leading restaurants adopted cabarets—live acts and bands. Special rooms for private dancing were available, and these contributed to the launch of various dance crazes endemic to Times Square. Nightclubs dedicated to the "midnight frolic," as Flo Ziegfeld called his popular cabaret, took over where these

BLUE PLATE *Specials*

clubs and restaurants left off. During World War I, nightlife in Times Square was severely impinged by two dubious milestones of American law: In 1917, Prohibition came in the Eighteenth Amendment to the Constitution, and in 1919 the Volstead Act enabled government agents to enforce it. Since Times Square was conceived in large part as a social and cultural alternative to unbending Victorian morals, the ban on intoxicants—a war on urban mores by Protestant temperance advocates and "reformers"—altered the ecology of the Square and encouraged its bottom-feeders to rise to the surface. The demand for alcohol surpassed the need for sobriety, and by 1925 hundreds of speakeasies were situated in Times Square. Later came clip-joints, where unsuspecting rubes wanting a good time were fleeced of their cash. With Repeal in 1933, Times Square turned again. Entrepreneurs were encouraged to break free from the gangster grips that Prohibition had fostered. In the years before World War II, criminal elements were rousted, and restaurant and café society saw a renaissance that continued until the sixties.

[PREVIOUS PAGE]

CONGA RESTAURANT

Detail from Menu
C.1950

SARDI'S

This landmark of the Theater District, founded in 1921, has long been known as a dining and watering hole for Broadway personalities. Here they would meet after a premiere to wait for notices from New York's legendary critics.

Menu and Ashtray

C. 1 9 4 8

Buffet Froid

STUFFED TOMATO SURPRISE with Chicken or Tunafish 3.75   with Shrimp 4.25

with Lump Crabmeat 4.75   with Lobster 5.75

ALLIGATOR PEAR STUFFED with Shrimp 4.25   with Crabmeat 4.75   with Lobster 5.75

LUMP CRABMEAT REMOULADE with Cole Slaw 4.75

HALF LOBSTER with Vegetable Salad a la Russe 4.50

SALMON STEAK with Vegetable Salad and Sauce Remoulade 3.50

CHEF'S SALAD, Garni 2.75   CAESAR SALAD 2.75

CHICKEN SALAD 3.50   SHRIMP SALAD 4.25   FRUIT SALAD 2.75

LUMP CRABMEAT SALAD 4.75   LOBSTER SALAD 5.75

TARTAR STEAK with Anchovy, Egg, Capers, Onion Rings and Tomato 6.95

SLICED STEAK with Tomato Slice and Boston Lettuce 3.75

CHICKEN AND TONGUE in Aspic 3.50

SLICED CORNED BEEF AND IMPORTED SWISS CHEESE, Cole Slaw 3.50

SLICED CHICKEN AND HAM with Waldorf Salad 3.50

ASSORTED COLD CUTS with Potato Salad 3.50

(There is an Extra Charge for a Single Portion served for Two)

Sardi's

... French Imports from Bordeaux ...

		Bouteille	Demi
29	CHATEAU HAUT BRION, Grave, White	8.50	
30	CHATEAU D'YQUEM	10.00	
31	SAUTERNES, Jouvet	5.00	3.00
32	CHATEAU HAUT BRION, Grave, Red	12.00	
33	CHATEAU MARGAUX	9.75	
34	GRAND VIN DE CHATEAU LATOUR	12.00	
35	CHATEAU PONTET CANET	6.50	3.75
36	CHATEAU AUSONE ST. EMILION	9.75	
37	CHATEAU TALBOT ST. JULIEN	6.00	3.50
38	CHATEAU MOUTON ROTHSCHILD MEDOC	12.00	6.50
39	CHATEAU CHEVAL BLANC, ST. EMILION	9.75	

... French Imports from Burgundy ...

40	MEURSAULT, Estate Bottling	5.50	3.00
41	CHABLIS, Jouvet	6.00	3.50
42	BATARD MONTRACHET, Estate Bottling	8.75	
43	POUILLY FUISSE, Jouvet	5.50	3.00
44	BEAUJOLAIS, Jouvet	4.75	2.75
45	POMMARD, Jouvet	6.75	3.75
46	GEVREY CHAMBERTIN, Estate Bottling	7.00	3.50
47	RICHEBOURG, Estate Bottling	10.00	
48	NUIT ST. GEORGE, Estate Bottling	8.00	
49	ALOXE CORTON, Estate Bottling	10.00	

... Moselle and Rhine Wines ...

MOSELLE

50	BERNKASTELER		
51	PIESPORTER GOLDTROEPFCHEN	5.50	3.00
52	WEHLENER SONNENUHR	6.50	

RHINE

53	HOCHHEIMER KONIGIN VICTORIA BERG	5.50	3.00
54	JOHANNISBERGER SCHLOSSBERG	5.50	
55	BLUE NUN LIEBFRAUMILCH, Superior, Extra Dry	6.50	3.75

... Italian Wines ...

60	ORVIETO, LUIGI BIGI, White	4.75	2.75
61	FRECCIAROSSA, White	4.75	2.75
62	CHIANTI RUFFINO, Red	4.75	2.75
63	CHIANTI BROLIO, Red	4.75	2.75
64	BARDOLINO, Red	4.75	2.75
65	SOAVE, White	4.75	
66	VALPOLICELLA, Red	4.75	2.75
67	VERDICCHIO, White	4.75	
68	CHIANTI, RESERVA DUCALE, Red	5.25	

SE ASK YOUR CAPTAIN FOR THE VINTAGES AVAILABLE

1626 Broadway
at Fiftieth Street
New York

Lindy's INC.

1655 Broadway
at Fifty-first Street
New York

COCKTAILS

FROZEN DAIQUIRI, WEST INDIES STYLE .... .65

DRY MARTINI made with Gordon's Gin and Imported Vermouth .... .60
BACARDI made with Bacardi ...... .55   FINE PALE DRY SHERRY WITH DUBONNET .. .35
BETWEEN THE SHEETS .... .75   ALEXANDER wth Creme de Cacao and Brandy .. .75

MANHATTAN	.60	EL PRESIDENTE	.60	DAIQUIRI	.60
SWEET MARTINI	.65	WARD EIGHT	.75	PANAMA	.70
OLD FASHIONED	.65	CARUSO	.65	DOCTOR	.70
EMPIRE	.60	CORONATION	.65	SIDE CAR	.70
ORANGE BLOSSOM	.60	CLOVER CLUB	.70	DUBONNET	.60
BRONX	.60	ROB ROY	.75	COFFEE	.75
LONE TREE	.60	CLOVER LEAF	.70	STINGER	.75
JACK ROSE	.60	PINK LADY	.70	BRANDY	.75
BLUE MOON	.60	WHITE LADY	.70	PERNOD	.75
HAVANA	.60	SAZERAC	.70	PICK-ME-UP	.75

Scotch Mist ..65   Scotch on the Rocks 65   Scotch Old Fashioned 75

WELCH'S CONCORD GRAPE WINE 25c. with Split of White Rock 10c. Extra

CUBA LIBRE .60   TOM COLLINS .... .60   RUM COLLINS .... .65

HARVEY'S BRISTOL MILK SHERRY ...65

HARVEY'S DRY AMONTILLADO SHERRY ...35

BERRY BROS. FINEST CREAM SHERRY ...55

Imported Pedro Domecq Pale Dry Fragrant 30c.

WHISKIES

RYES AND BOURBONS

	Drink 1½ oz.
SEAGRAM'S 7 CROWN	55
Gallagher & Burton White Label	" " 50
Hiram Walker Imperial	" " 50
Hiram Walker De Luxe	" " 55
Park & Tilford Reserve	" " 55
Schenley Reserve	" " 55
Lord Calvert	" " 55
Four Roses	" " 55
Carstairs White Seal	" " 55
Park & Tilford Private Stock	" " 60
Southern Comfort	" " 65

Bonded Rye and Bourbon Whiskies

County Fair, 4 yrs. old	" " 55
Kentucky Tavern Bonded, 4 yrs. old	" " 55
Park & Tilford, Bottled in Bond, 4 yrs. old	" " 60
Seagram's V. O., 6 yrs. old	" " 65
Hiram Walker's Canadian Club	" " 65
Old Schenley, 8 yrs. old	" " 65
I. W. Harper Bourbon, 4 yrs. old	" " 65
Old Joe, 7 yrs. old	" " 65
Bonded Beam, 7 yrs. old	" " 65
Pebbleford Kentucky Bourbon, 7 yrs. old	" " 65
Cave Hollow, 8 yrs. old	" " 65
Old Taylor, 4 yrs. old	" " 65
Old Grand-Dad, 4 yrs. old	" " 65
MOUNT VERNON, 13 yrs. old	" " 95

SCOTCH

	Drink 1½ oz.
CUTTY SARK	65
House of Lords	" " 65
Ballantine's	" " 65
Bell's Special Reserve	" " 65
Campbell's	" " 65
Grand Macnish	" " 65
White Horse Cellar	" " 65
Haig & Haig *****	" " 65
Gilbey's Spey Royal	" " 65
Dewar's White Label	" " 65
Black & White	" " 65
Usher's Green Stripe	" " 65
Johnnie Walker, Red Label	" " 65
Vat 69	" " 65
King's Ransom	" " 75
St. James	" " 75
Haig & Haig, Pinch Bottle	" " 85
Johnnie Walker, Black Label	" " 85
Old Rarity	" " 85

Aged Scotch Whiskies

Lang's, 8 yrs. old	" " 65
Mackinlay's, 8 yrs. old	" " 65
Ambassador, 12 yrs. old	" " 75
Chivas Regal, 12 yrs. old	" " 95
Bell's, 12 yrs. old	" " 1.10
Martins de Luxe, 12 yrs. old	" " 1.10
OLD SMUGGLER, 18 yrs. old	" " 1.10
Bell's Royal Reserve, 20 yrs. old	" " 1.25
Ballantine's, 25 yrs. old	" " 1.25
AMBASSADOR, 25 yrs. old	" " 1.25
Ripe Old Age, 27 yrs. old	" " 1.25

Individual Ginger Ale or White Rock Served Free of Charge with Highball

WHISKEY SOUR 75   RUM SOUR   65   SCOTCH SOUR 85

BRANDIES AND COGNACS

	Pony	Drink
B. & B. BENEDICTINE AND REMY MARTIN BRANDY	75	1.10
MARTELL *** CORDON BLEU, 80 yrs. old, served in Bouquet Glass		1.45
MARTELL CORDON ARGENT, 80 yrs. old, served in Bouquet Glass		1.65

	Pony	Drink		Pony	Drink
Martell ***	55	95	Otard, VSOP	75	1.10
Hine	55	95	COURVOISIER V. S.	75	1.10
Berry Bros. ****	55	95	Drambuie	75	1.10
Bisquit Dubouche	55	95	Remy Martin, VSOP	75	1.10
Hennessy ***	55	95	Hildick's Apple Brandy, 5 yrs. old		60

DINNER 1655

SEE SPECIAL WINE LIST

[OPPOSITE]

LINDY'S

This former landmark eatery was called
Mindy's in the Damon Runyon stories about
Broadway. As Lindy's, it was world famous
for its incomparable cheesecake.

Menu
1953

A LA CARTE

Times Square was a menu capital. Billy
Rose's Diamond Horseshoe in the Hotel
Paramount (top right) was a draw, as was the
International Theater Restaurant (top left)
and Rector's (bottom right, c.1901)

Menus
C.1940S

"The Meeting Place of the W...
Jack Dempsey's Broadway I...

JACK DEMPSEY'S RESTAURANT

JACK DEMPSEYS

ACK DEMPSEY'S GRILL

JACK'S

JACK DEMPS
BROADWAY I
and
COCKTAIL LOU...
BROADWAY
"The Meeting Place of the World"

The Lobster
145 W. 45TH St.
NEW YORK
CITY.
MAX FUCHS & SIMON LINZ

YOUR HOST
D. L. TOFFENETTI

CROSSROADS
Bar · Restaurant · Cafe

MELTED CHEESE SANDWICH	CHOPPED BEEFSTEAK	FRIJID SALAD BOWL	CROSSROADS COLLINS
with Beechnut Bacon or Grilled Tomato, India Relish	Smothered with Onions	Fresh Spring Vegetables, Tossed Lightly, Garnished with Julienne of Chicken, Hard Boiled Egg, Roquefort or Russian Dressing	Made with Seagram's Ancient Gin, Served in a Tall Glass with a Stick of Fresh Fruit and Mint, Raspberry and Club Soda
35¢	Made of Freshly Chopped Prime Beef, Served with Fresh Vegetable and Fried Potatoes 75¢	85¢	45¢

Toffenetti RESTAURANT
FAMOUS FOR HAM and SWEETS
43rd and Broadway ♥ In the Heart of Times Square
The Busiest Restaurant on the World's Busiest Corner
New York City

Toffenetti
RESTAURANT

BROADWAY
42ND ST. TIMES SQUARE 7TH AVE.

An Eating Place at the Meeting Place of the World

AUTOMAT
HORN & HARDART
HORN & HARDART

Good morning
Toffenetti can please your morning appetite

Toffenetti
RESTAURANT
43rd & BROADWAY · ON TIMES SQUA...

"THE SHOW PLACE OF NEW YORK"

— says Harper's Bazaar

"MOST SPECTACULAR CAFE REVUE BROADWAY HAS EVER SEEN" (Leonard Lyons, Post)

INTERNATIONAL CASINO New York City

44th to 45th Sts. on B'way

Top Hats LEAD THE WAY TO The Rainbow Room

RAY NOBLE and his orchestra

MILLY MONTI
toast of the Continent—American debut

ENRICA and NOVELLO
in new variations of the dance

EDGAR BERGEN
urbane ventriloquist

NANO RODRIGO
and his tango-rhumba band

For Distinguished Dining and Dancing
6:30 until 3 A. M. nightly, except Sunday
Reservations: Circle 6-1400

ROCKEFELLER CENTER RO

There's an air of hospitality that you'll like

AT THE HOTEL

PICCADILLY

227 WEST 45TH STREET
· AT BROADWAY ·

NEW YORK

· · ·

ADJACENT TO EVERY ACTIVITY
600 BRIGHT, SUNLIT ROOMS
EACH WITH BATH
ELECTRIC FAN
ICE WATER

SINGLE ROOM AND BATH $300

DOUBLE ROOM AND BATH $450

EXCEPTIONAL RESTAURANT AND GRILLE

WIRE AT JOUR EXPENSE FOR RESERVATIONS

F. D. SOFIELD MANAGING DIR.

"THE MOST MAGNIFICENT NIGHT CLUB PRESENTATION I'VE EVER SEEN"

Ed Sullivan DAILY NEWS

SHOW
Clifford C. Fischer's Sensational
FOLIES d'AMOUR
On the Cocktail Lounge
An Intimate Revue

★

DINING
Unexcelled Cuisine
Table d'Hote Dinner
6:30 to 10 P. M.
Supper 10 P. M. to closing

★

DANCING
to 3 Orchestras
Vincent Travers
Art Shaw
Eddie South

Reservations:
COI. 5-7070

French Casino

7th Avenue and 50th St.

THE WORLD'S MOST FAMOUS THEATRE-RESTAURANT

LA CONGA

A Corner of Havana In N.Y.

57 W. 57th ST.
PLaza 5-5757

DICK GASPARRE
And His Orchestra

LA CONGA ORCHESTRA
with Hilda Salazar

EL CANEY QUARTETTE
AT THE BAR

NO COUVERT

THEATER,
DINING, DANCING

The French Casino, Piccadilly,
International Casino, Rainbow
Room, and La Conga helped
give the Theater District its
unique allure as a nightspot.

Advertisements
c. 1940s

Paradise Girls

Gorgeous! Glamorous! Thrilling!

PARADISE CABARET RESTAURANT, 49th St & Broadway, New York City

PARADISE GIRLS

As advertised, they were gorgeous, glamorous, and thrilling. They were also the stars of one of Times Square's many caberets.

Brochure
1935

[OPPOSITE]

JACK'S, TOOTS'S, AND MORE

These matchbooks advertised everything for the nightbird, from Dempsey's storied eatery to the China Garden restaurant (Times Square was known for its fine Cantonese food).

Matchbooks
C. 1930S-40S

AUTHENTIC
Cuban-Spanish
Atmosphere

NIGHTLY SHOWS
7.45 12.00 2.15

CIrcle 6-7258

La Conga

51st STREET
AT BROADWAY
NEW YORK

CLOSE COVER BEFORE STRIKING

Jack Dempsey's
RESTAURANT

BAR and GRILL
8TH AVENUE AT 50TH ST.
NEW YORK CITY

OPPOSITE MADISON SQUARE GARDEN

Come in
and say hello!

Yours Truly
Jack Dempsey

CLOSE COVER BEFORE STRIKING

ADMINISTRATION BUILDING

NEW YORK WORLD'S FAIR

FOOD AT ITS BEST

FOR THE FINEST
NEW YORK "FARE"

CHINA
GARDEN

CHINESE & AMERICAN
RESTAURANT
136 WEST 50th STREET
NEW YORK

CLOSE COVER BEFORE STRIKING

FEDERAL MATCH CORP., NEW YORK

RKO THEATRES
AT ALL

ENJOY
AMERICA'S BEST CANDY
A·B

ALWAYS A
BETTER SHOW
AT RKO

RKO
THEATRES

THE Best
IN ENTERTAINMENT

CLOSE COVER BEFORE STRIKING

LION MATCH Co. Inc. N.Y. MADE IN U.S.A.

RESTAURANT

51 W. 51 St.

TOOTS SHOR

PLAZA 3-9000

TOOTS
SHOR
51 W. 51 St.
New York

CLOSE COVER BEFORE STRIKING

BRYANT 9-8738

TIMES SQUARE
NEW YORK CITY

Paramount THEATRE

WHERE EVERY DAY
IS A HOLIDAY

THE HOME OF Paramount PICTURES

BROADWAY'S BIGGEST
STAGE AND SCREEN SHOW

PARAMOUNT

THEATRE

FEATURE MATCH BOOK PAT. 1,639,845-6
LION MATCH Co., Inc. N.Y. MADE IN U.S.A.

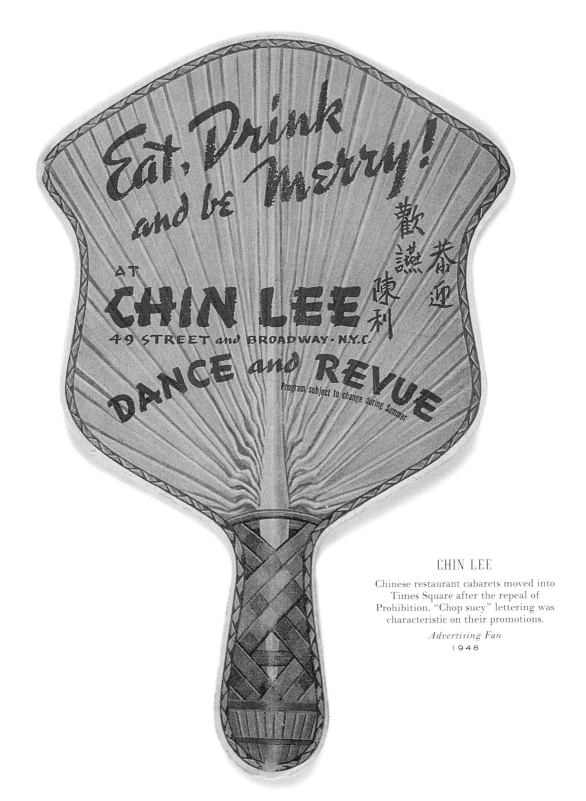

CHIN LEE

Chinese restaurant cabarets moved into
Times Square after the repeal of
Prohibition. "Chop suey" lettering was
characteristic on their promotions.

Advertising Fan
1948

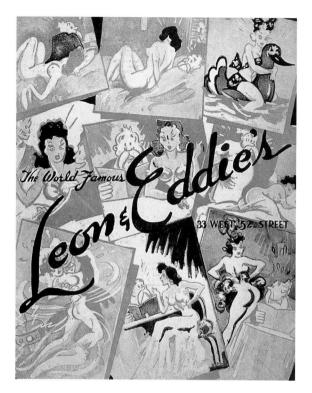

LEON & EDDIE'S

This wartime menu admonished,
"Eat well, but without waste," and
"Food will win the war."

Menu
1945

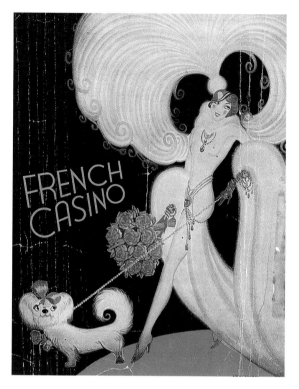

FRENCH CASINO

The chic illustration belied the fact
that this gambling-free casino did not
appeal to the upper crust.

Menu
C. 1935

VARIOUS RESTAURANT AND CABARET INTERIORS

Postcards
1908–45

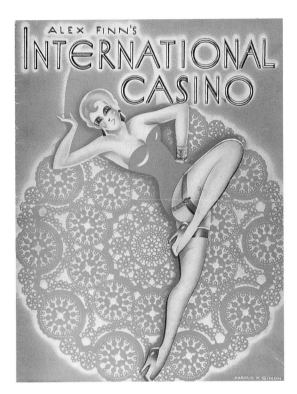

INTERNATIONAL CASINO

Known for its showgirls in various stages of undress, Finn's was the epitome of luxe and swank, a glittering amalgam of crystal fountains, revolving stages, and a three-story spiral bar. A 1936 guidebook called it "a Hollywood dream... with an elaborate musical revue."

Menu
1936

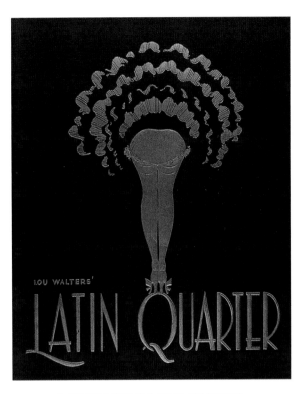

LOU WALTER'S LATIN QUARTER

Its slogan read: "As much a part of New York as Broadway." Stars such as Martin & Lewis, Sophie Tucker, and Frank Sinatra played there.

Souvenir Book
C. 1954

LEON & EDDIE'S

Like other nightspots on Times Square, Leon
& Eddie's was not shy about generating
publicity in the gauchest ways possible.

Matchbooks

C.1947

Souvenirs are artless by design, and the trinkets for sale in Times Square's souvenir shops are no exception. These postcards, pennants, and baubles have much in common with kitschy works of ephemera that commemorate other locales, yet by virtue of the Times Square imprimatur those included here have a bit more panache. Indeed, a souvenir may on rare occasions—when its graphic elements are cleverly devised and aesthetically composed—transcend cliché. The modernistic, somewhat abstract handkerchief design on page 138 (a reductive version of the postcard tableau on the cover of this book) is a case in point. By virtue of its artful simplicity, it possesses a distinct charm that extends beyond its commercial function. It may have been produced in large quantity, but it does not mimic the cookie-cutter version on the opposite page. At the risk of hyperbole endemic to Times Square itself, we might say that this artifact documents the tension between old and new, and high and low Broadway culture—at

a cost of only fifty cents. Most souvenirs imprint a recollection, even if the person holding it did not actually partake in the thing being recollected. The souvenirs in this section bare little resemblance to the Times Square that exists today, but they are an imprint of the iconic place it once was. Even cigarette and tobacco packages contribute to the legend. Also included here are a collection of pulp hardback and paperback covers, mysteries mostly, recalling the slightly off-color underbelly of Broadway life, real and imagined. They are shown here as readers of these volumes were doubtless transported into the mythic reality that is the essence of the souvenir. *Terror in Times Square* may not be the precise image that the Square's impresarios would have chosen for it, but it does vividly capture the darker caste of the area. Conversely, *The Broadway Melody* suggests a brighter vision. But nothing captures the contrasts of Times Square better than the image on *Broadway Murders*, with its lively chorus girls set against a backdrop of crime.

[PREVIOUS PAGE}

BRIDE FROM BROADWAY

Wesley Snyder
Book Cover
1951

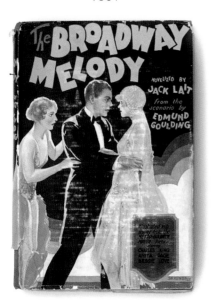

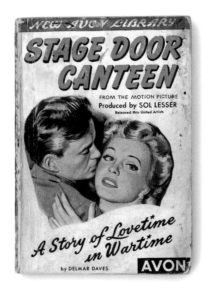

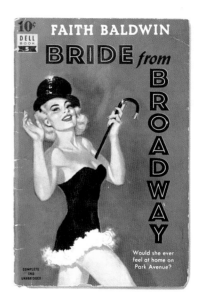

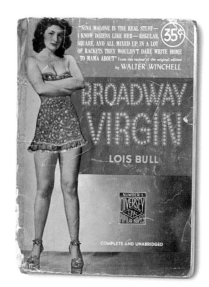

PULP FICTIONS

Broadway was the inspiration for movies,
music, and of course literature of the
sordid sort. Even Damon Runyon focused
on the seedier side of Times Square.

Paperback and Hardback Covers.
1929–51

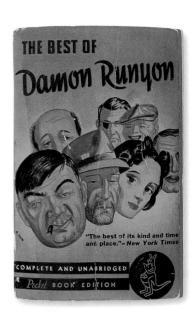

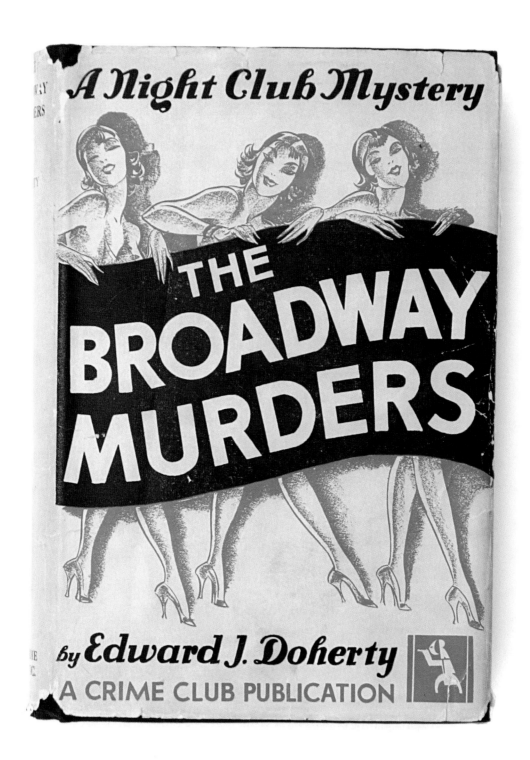

A Night Club Mystery

THE BROADWAY MURDERS

by Edward J. Doherty

A CRIME CLUB PUBLICATION

c. 1955

NEW YORK, NEW YORK

These hankies are impressions of the square; the one on the
right is more abstract than the sketchy version on the left, but
both portray the quintessential Time Square.

Souvenir Handkerchief

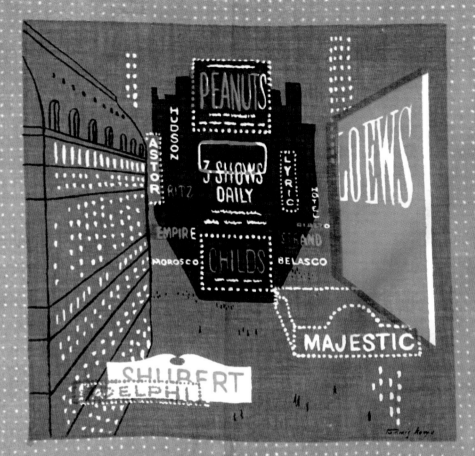

c. 1960

DINTY MOORE'S

This is one of the Times Square bars that encouraged its patrons
to walk away with a small remembrance of drinks past.

Cocktail Glass

C.1950

[OPPOSITE]

TIMES SQUARE CIGARETTES

According to the National Leaf Tobacco Corp.,
the "people's choice" was Times Square.

Cigarette Carton

C.1928

[OPPOSITE]

TIMES SQUARE
SMOKING MIXTURE

This pipe tobacco tin was one of many
souvenirs designed to make a visitor an
addict of Times Square.

Tobacco Tin

C.1920

Bibliography

Baral, Robert. *Revue*. New York, Fleet Press Corporation, 1962.

Bloom, Ken. *Broadway: An Encylopedic Guide to the History, People and Places of Times Square*. New York, Facts on File, 1991.

Durante, Jimmy, and Jack Kofoed. *Night Clubs*. New York, Alfred A. Knopf, 1931.

Elliot, Marc. *Down 42nd Street*. New York, Warner Books, 2001.

Granlund, Nils T. *Blondes, Brunettes and Bullets*. New York, Van Rees Press, 1957.

Kennedy, Rod. *Lost New York in Old Postcards*. Salt Lake City, Gibbs Smith, 2001.

Lankevich, George J. *Postcards from Times Square*. Garden City, NY, Square One Publishers, 2001.

Lass, William. *Crossroads of the World: The Story of Times Square*. New York, Popular Library, 1965.

Lewis, Stephen. *Hotel Kid*. Philadelphia, Paul Dry Books, 2002.

Rogers, W. G., and Mildred Weston. *Carnival Crossroads: The Story of Times Square*. Garden City, NY, Doubleday & Company, Inc., 1960.

Shaw, Charles G. *NightLife*. New York, The John Day Company, 1931.

Stone, Jill. *Times Square: A Pictorial History*. New York, Collier Books, 1982.

Taylor, William. *Inventing Times Square*. Baltimore, The Johns Hopkins University Press, 1991.

Traub, James. *The Devil's Playground*. New York, Random House, 2004.

Wagoner, Susan. *Nightclub Nights*. New York, Rizzoli International Publications, 2001.

Times Square Bldg.,
New York.

Acknowledgments

This book would have been impossible without the interest and enthusiasm of Mark Lamster, our editor at Princeton Architectural Press, or the design and art direction of Louise Fili and Chad Roberts at Louise Fili Ltd., New York. Thank you all.

Further thanks for the inspiration, encouragement, and shared memories of Times Square and Broadway from Ken Anthony, Linda Arking and Robert Avila, Barbara Cohen, Marilyn and Alvin Cooperman, Lisa Fiel, Leonard Finger, Kees Gajentaan, Andrew Garn, John Gilman, Evelyn Goldberg, Fred Goldberg, Wendall K. Harrington, Robert Heide, Trudy Kaplan, Rod Kennedy, Margaret Knapp, Laura Kreiss, Barry Lewis, Ron Lieberman, Gloria Loomis, Tom Mellins, Richard Merkin, Phyllis Newman, Max Page, Fred Papert, Bibi Neezamodeen Pardo, Kenn Rabin, Vincent Sardi, Jr., Gerry Schoenfeld, Arthur Schwartz, Nanette Smith, Richard Snow, Ellen Stern, Henry Voigt; and in memorium for cherished conversations with Seymour Durst, Adolph Green, Douglas Leigh, Doc Pomus, Tiny Tim, Arthur Tracy, and Doris Vinton of the Ziegfeld Follies — all legends of Times Square.

We are greatful for the input and cooperation of the following individuals and institutions: Tom Bodkin; Mirko Ilić; Mike Bornstein AKA Dr. Kolmo, magician; Madeline Castellotti, Peter Castellotti, John's Pizza; Richard Cohn, magic historian; Eric Concklin, archivist, Ziegfeld Club; Phillip Copp and Larry Furlong, Electric Railroaders Association; Harriet Culver, Allen Reuben, and Eva Tucholka, Culver Pictures; David Graveen/Popcorn Posters; Kathryn Hausman, director of the Art Deco Society of New York; Susan Kim and Rachael Wright, Corbis; Tom Klem, artist/historian; KJA consulting, Orlando, Fla.; Miles Krueger, Institute of the American Musical; Cathy Leff, executive director, Marianne Lamonaca, assistant curator, and Francis Luca, librarian of the Wolfsonian - Florida State University, Miami Beach; Howard and Ron Mandlebaum, Photofest; Jeremy Merrin, Havana Central; Metropolitan Postcard Club; Jon Oliver, magician; Bruce Stapleton, Playbill, Inc.; Jan Ramirez, director, Holly Hinman, assistant curator of photographs, Kathleen Hulser, public historian, and Mary Beth Kavanagh, director of rights & reproduction of the New-York Historical Society; Brett Sirota, the Road Company; Mark Swartz, Shubert Archive; Tim Topkins, president of the Times Square Alliance; Miriam K. Tierney, archivist, New York Transit Museum; and the amazing ebay online community.

Our gratitude to Rebecca Bartlett at Louise Fili Ltd. for her production assistance. We also appreciate the work of Leo Barnes of Printing Express; Tony Cencicola for his photography; Kevin Downs; Louis Laureano, Hardy Rothstein, and Dennis Lyn at Jellybean Photographics and Imaging; and Larry Mohle of C D & L Messenger Service.

Thanks also to Kevin Lippert, publisher, as well as Nettie Aljian, Penny Chu, Russell Fernandez, and Katharine Smalley at Princeton Architectural Press.

And a special hug to Adam, Alex and Ollie Levi, who made room in their lives for the historical annals of Times Square Style. VGL & SH